Parents Who Have Only One Child Face a Unique Challenge

In this intelligent and practical book,
Dr. Murray Kappelman, a leading pediatrician,
shows that the only child does not have to
be the self-absorbed, overprivileged child of
popular myth *if* parents are prepared for
the pressures and pitfalls and learn to avoid
them. He explains the whole range of potential
problems and provides clear and direct
prescriptions for raising a healthy only child
from infancy to young adulthood.

- **Isolation and loneliness**
- **Peer relationships**
- **Early maturity or prolonged immaturity**
- **Insecurities and dependency problems**
- **Learning to share**
- **The adopted only child**
- **Dealing with divorce and death**
- **And much, much more**

SIGNET Books of Special Interest to Parents

☐ **FAMILY COMMUNICATION by Sven Wahlroos, Ph.D.** The essential guide for achieving more effective, harmonious relationships, including 20 rules to improve communications and make your relationships more loving, supportive and enriching, and 10 essential characteristics of emotional health, and how to achieve them.
(#J7067—$1.95)

☐ **THE HALF-PARENT by Brenda Maddox.** The vital guide to more satisfying stepparent-stepchild relationships . . . "Excellent . . . all the hazards and the solutions." —Gesell Institute of Child Development
(#E7214—$1.75)

☐ **HOW TO PARENT by Fitzhugh Dodson.** A revolutionary new approach to your child's formative years that puts joy back in parenthood and discipline back in child-rearing. (#E7716—$2.25)

☐ **HOW TO FATHER by Dr. Fitzhugh Dodson.** "Any man will be a better father after reading this book. . . . From diapers to drugs, from the beginning of self-awareness to adolescent sexuality, from infancy to teens, it's ALL here . . . the most comprehensive and useful book on child-raising I have ever read."—Dr. Louise Bates Ames, Co-Director, Gesell Institute of Child Development
(#E8416—$2.50)

☐ **YOUR CHILD FROM ONE TO TWELVE. Introduction by Dr. Lee Salk.** For concerned parents, this volume is a guidebook to help them prepare their children for the world in which they are growing up. The companion volume to this is **Your Child in Adolescence.**
(#E8421—$1.75)

If you wish to order these titles, please see the coupon in the back of this book.

RAISING THE ONLY CHILD

by

Murray Kappelman, M.D.

A SIGNET BOOK

NEW AMERICAN LIBRARY

TIMES MIRROR

Library of Congress Catalog Card Number: 74-31416

This is an authorized reprint of a hardcover edition published by
E. P. Dutton & Co., Inc. The hardcover edition was published
simultaneously in Canada by Clarke, Irwin & Company Limited,
Toronto and Vancouver.

A small portion of this work was first published in *Glamour* Magazine
in considerably different form.

To my wife, Joan,
another important only child

Contents

1

Why the Only Child?

WHEN I WAS GROWING up as an only child, my parents constantly made excuses for this situation. My mother would flush and whisper of her difficulty in having more children. Miscarriage followed miscarriage as she tried to meet both her personal needs and society's demand that she rear more than one child. In previous generations, extended families lived in close proximity: grandparents, aunts, uncles, cousins, and siblings. If they did not share the same house, it was not uncommon for them to share the same street or neighborhood. They gathered often to make family decisions, to celebrate family joys or to mourn losses, and to reaffirm the bonds that held them together, safe, insulated, and protected from the rapidly changing, often hostile outside world. The extended family was its own internal society, greatly influencing many decisions and life patterns of the married couples living within it. This tight extended family society generally frowned on the rearing of an only child, indicating that the process was selfish, wasteful, contrary to the prevailing concept of the large family, and intrinsically threatening to the ultimate survival of the total family as a functioning protective body.

The larger society beyond the borders of the family also frowned upon the concept of only-child rearing. Social agencies had predetermined policies that refused to allow single-child adoptions. Only children were viewed by the behaviorally oriented professional community as having two strikes against them. This belief was not confined to professional journals or scientific conferences but was commonly held, written about copiously in popular magazines, and accepted as fact in daily conversation. Most only children were pitied; they were prisoners of a rearing situation that had a very high likelihood of pathologic outcomes.

As I confronted the normal problems of mischievous behavior or acting out what any growing boy would experience, I'd hear the neighbors comment: "Well, you know, he's an only child." This became so threatening that a family who might have wanted to rear only one child often reluctantly had more in order to avoid the stigma and the shame of having the audacity to attempt the upbringing of a single youngster.

Times have changed dramatically. Significant shifts in lifestyles and philosophies have occurred, and the rearing of an only child is rapidly becoming a common pattern in this country. According to the 1972 census, 18.9 percent of families in the United States had only one child under eighteen years of age living within their family unit. This includes older families with grown children, but a significant proportion of these families are those with but one child. The same census revealed that approximately 8.7 million families had one child under six years of age. These families have a high probability of remaining only-child families or of having children so widely spaced as to have the equivalent of two "only" children in one household. I predict that this trend will continue and that at some point in the future, the United States will have a high percentage of only children.

Why? There has been a gradual but distinct dissolution of the extended family. The tight ethnic neighborhoods of urban areas and the clustered rural family units have generally broken up and have been replaced by movements from cities into suburbs and from rural settings into urban communities. Distances between members of families have widened. Older members of families, with later retirement and social security, tend to live less and less with their children. Families are also increasingly mobile as job opportunities open in other cities far from the hometown. Today's young married couple is much more likely to make a move for career advancement than was the couple of twenty-five or thirty years ago. Therefore, the close-knit extended family has disassembled, rarely gathering as a large unit except for major events—traditional holidays, weddings, anniversaries, funerals. Young couples today cluster not around original families, but primarily with their own social and age groups. The extended adult peer group has in many cases replaced the extended family, and such social units are more likely to provide positive reinforcement of a young couple's decision to have a single child.

One of the most significant features of this changing society is the emergence of the woman as an individual in her own right. Society has finally begun to break down the stereotypic roles of husband and wife with the clear-cut constraints that these narrow definitions place upon each of the partners. A woman no longer has to limit her horizons to a kitchen, an apron, a baby bottle, diapers, and the transportation of children back and forth from their music lessons and schools. Young girls today learn early that there is nothing they cannot attain if it lies within their physical and intellectual capability. Young women have accepted the challenge with refreshing vigor. They are entering new fields, competing successfully with men in almost all the professions, and soon will have kicked over the final barriers in the very few occupations that remain partially closed. Colleges are flooded with older women returning to school, or to work toward master's and doctorate degrees, all aimed toward the full realization of a productive and creative career. But where, in the struggle for career, degree, self-actualization, is the function of childbearing and child-rearing? Obviously, the couple must plan carefully and decide how many children can be accommodated into their lives. Some decide that they will forgo parenting entirely, that they will not be caught in the "baby trap," as Ellen Peck has described it. Instead, they dedicate themselves and their marriage to the full attainment of their separate careers and independence. Many more, however, will not wish to give up the experience of parenthood, which they perceive as an important and integral facet of marriage. But because of the pressures of time, schooling, and job opportunities, the couple recognizes that to successfully accomplish both career and parenting, they must limit themselves to a single child. They realize that, if done with insight and informed preparation, the rearing of a single child can be both exciting and innovative as well as creative work. The active, career-oriented mother and father perceive that it is the quality, not the quantity, of parenting that is essential. Therefore, the trend toward only-child family commonly blends in with the liberated, career-directed woman and the educated, upwardly mobile man who finds such a partner more of a stimulation than a threat.

Another reason for the increase in only-child families is the easier accessibility of both male and female contraceptives today. Religious barriers, although mostly unchanged, have not always prevented couples from making the choice between their religious sect's beliefs and their independent lives. A couple may well decide on a large family for religious reasons, but in most cases, today's young couple will have given the alternatives some consideration. And well they should. These decisions should be based on belief, not dictum, on religious dedication, not passive acceptance of inert rules. With the availability of high-quality, highly effective contraceptive devices, the chances of an unwanted pregnancy are much less than they were in the past. Legalized abortion in many states has further emphasized the concept of choice in family planning. A young couple can systematically plan for their single child and usually have it when they want it.

Raising a child in an inflationary economy can be financially difficult and frustrating. To provide a child with the proper home environment that permits free play, peer companionship, and a safe street environment often means buying a suburban home. The larger the family, the bigger and more expensive the home. Clothing the child can be as expensive as clothing the adult. Parents with vision clearly see the implications of schooling in today's society for their future children. If they are fortunate to live in a community with satisfactory public education, they will pay dearly for it in the cost of their home or apartment. If they attempt to economize in their home buying or staunchly support the concept of urban living for themselves and their youngster, they may likely be forced to consider private school if they demand high-quality education. Such costs are a very serious consideration when a young couple carefully examines the alternatives to the number and timing of their future family. To many, then, an only child is a financial necessity.

Social agencies have also reassessed their positions. For instance, the adoption of children has become a highly competitive and selective process due to the dwindling baby supply caused by more diversified, better distributed and more readily available methods of birth control, plus the availability of abortion without parental consent in some states. So adoption agencies which once looked with concern at the family who wanted to adopt a single child and strongly advised and crusaded against such a practice, today may be forced to accept the only-child adoption because of the unavailability of infants to create the two- or three-child unit. To permit more families who have problems in natural parenthood to experience the joys of child-rearing, the adoption establishment may ultimately be forced into a one-child-per-family philosophy.

There are adults who have realized honestly and with insight that they, as individuals, can manage the responsibilities and parental duties of only one child. They do not consider themselves inadequate as adults. It was only when society so pressured them that they succumbed unhappily to having more than one child or had the only child and hid the honesty of their reasons behind false excuses. Today the stigma of having the only child has been lifted. Parents who simply wish to rear one child can do so with less likelihood of social concern or shame.

There are, in addition, subliminal reasons for the increase in the number of single-child families. These factors may or may not be present in the young couple's conscious thinking, but they do play a role in the peripheral aspects of some decisions to have a single child. Namely, the divorce rate is soaring. One in three marriages ends so, and it is predicted that the percentage will be rising in future years. Faced with the possibility of future incompatibility and divorce, the young couple of today may subconsciously limit the number of children early in the marriage to test the strength and longevity of the union. Most young people are highly sensitive to the problems faced by children of divorced parents and wish to avoid that dilemma if at all possible. So the delay in child-bearing and the wide spacing of pregnancies and possible ultimate limitation of the family to one child may reflect an awareness of these unnerving statistics. The serious problems of preteens and adolescents, the knowledge that an emerging adult will depend a great deal upon the cumulative input of both parents, and their interaction with their firstborn, may also have a negative effect upon a couple's desire for a larger family. Faced with the temptations and influences of the social situation today, it is little wonder parents feel that a single child will allow them a greater ability to control and thus reassure the development of a healthy, adjusted young adult. Mobility is another factor that enters into the decision of family size. The career of either parent may require freedom of movement, and demand quick reaction to job opportunities. The smaller the family, the easier and less hesitant the move.

The stigma that was attached to having one child reflected specific, inherent problems that must be recognized and understood thoroughly by parents who want to raise a healthy, adjusted, socially aware, and productive only child. No one child will experience all the problems discussed in this book. But being informed about the whole spectrum of possible dangers will give parents a head start in raising their youngster to be living proof that the only child can be as normal and contented as any other kid on the block.

2

Parenting
the Only Child

THE BIRTH OF THE first child creates a unique shift in the dynamics of a marriage. What was once a union of two people, interdependent in some areas and independent in others, suddenly changes and becomes a nuclear family. The relationships of the characters in the script must be realigned, the set redesigned. Plans must now be made with the newborn in mind. Housing, educational resources, the availability of professional and baby-sitting help, and the accessibility of playmates must all be weighed as the couple considers their family's future. Decisions are no longer adult-oriented; they now have a new dimension. They have become child-centered to a major degree.

The shift is often quite dramatic. The realization of the total dependency of the new baby makes an indelible impression on the parents as they contemplate their new roles. Usually, they assume their new responsibilities with relish and, at times, almost compulsive endurance. This new baby within the new family unit is a challenge, a test that must be passed. If they should fail, their own child will testify to their incompetence as parents.

When we brought our first child home from the hospital, my wife (herself an only child) was suddenly faced with a crying infant girl, a husband on duty as a resident at a hospital far across town, and a hired nurse who took an afternoon break and never reappeared. Here was a baby crying for food, no milk in the refrigerator, and a new mother unable to make the necessary formula for her child. A frantic phone call to a harassed husband and the gracious and generous house call of a hospital nurse saved the day and my wife's sanity and provided my daughter with the bottle that quieted her. The baby was satisfied and was, of course, unaware of the terror and anguish that went into that warm, delicious bottle of milk. But my wife had faced the possibility of parental inadequacy and failure during that revealing moment. Even now she recalls, with humor and remembered pain, the days that followed, during which she attempted to rebuild self-confidence in her ability to be a responsible and adequate guardian of the new life that had been entrusted to her immediate care. No parent is immune to this feeling, but with the firstborn, the sense of the child's dependency may be exquisite, intense, and almost impossible to overcome, frightening and even paralyzing the young couple.

The firstborn receives the parents' maximum effort but with minimum experience. And at least for the first few years, it may pay the price of experimental parenting, for new parents are often inconsistent and uncertain. If motivated and observant, however, they learn from their mistakes. When the second child arrives, the nuclear family is no longer an adventure; it is a state of being that has been accepted and relaxed into. Natural shifts in attention gradually and subtly occur, so that the firstborn by necessity is encouraged to mature, to become somewhat independent, to receive discipline—all because of the presence of a new life demanding time and attention.

But what happens if the firstborn is the only born; if it is, by choice or by chance, an only child? Then, the parent has no cause or reason to shift immediate attention away from the child, and the interaction between parents and only child is maintained at maximum force throughout childhood and early adulthood. Such an interaction between two dedicated adults and a developing child is obviously fraught with dangers that could result in a seriously impaired relationship and in a child who is not properly prepared to cope with a world in which the spotlight often shifts to others.

ESTABLISHING CONSISTENT RULES AND DISCIPLINE

The key to a successful relationship between the only child and its parents is a clear understanding of the rules of the game. Each family has its own. Some are quite structured, with discipline frequently administered; others tend to be more permissive, with critical assessment of the child's behavior administered only in response to major infractions. Either method is quite satisfactory in the long run if the style of behavior expected from the child fits in with the parents' general style of living and if the parents agree completely on clear perimeters of acceptable behavior. The essence of success in any home is that rules *do* exist, no matter how loose or rigid.

Many parents have the mistaken notion that discipline weakens their child's love for them. Consequently, they shy away from setting limits, hoping to woo and win their toddler. This is futile and dangerous. Children will love parents whom they respect. Discipline administered according to the family's established rules is the first step toward gaining that respect and love.

As a family increases in size, the parents must necessarily establish order and structure; otherwise, there will be utter chaos. But such is not the case in the family where there is only one child. There are no other internal forces demanding that rules be established and subsequent discipline administered. Therefore, it is far too easy for the parents to avoid setting standards of behavior rather than face the unpleasant task of reinforcing these rules by meting out appropriate punishment for infractions. In such cases, the parents may be unaware of how inadequately prepared their child is to cope in our society until the youngster's behavior comes into conflict with the outside world. The parents of the only child must be very careful about setting the same realistic limits, restrictions, and rules that the parents of a large family must establish because society is, in essence, a large, chaotic, often disorganized family in which the growing child will need a fair degree of self-control and self-discipline if it is to survive.

Abuse of these family rules must have predetermined consequences. Quite simply, the child who has broken a rule must be disciplined. Disciplining children creates conflicts and concerns for most parents. How much punishment? How severe? How long? What form should it take? The parents of the only child have had no previous experience and therefore must be particularly careful to choose beforehand, and then to administer appropriately, the methods of discipline decided upon. The essential part of the process is a clearly defined set of consequences for deviations from the rules. These consequences must be fully understood, accepted as reasonable, and meted out with consistent quantity and quality. This is the basis of the child's adjustment and security both within the family and, eventually, within society as a whole. Lack of a consistent approach will result in a confused child who has no siblings to turn to, emulate, or observe in similar disciplinary situations.

Discipline should never be confused with love. To punish a child is in no way to diminish his regard for the parent; if anything, it tends to build his respect for parental authority and strength. Only unfair or unjust, excessive or weak, and inconsistent punishment breeds anger or contempt in the child. For the unschooled parent of the only child, the conflict is too often focused on the issue of discipline versus love. Once this conflict is understood and resolved, the only child can be disciplined fairly and appropriately, without fear of disrupting a warm and meaningful bond.

It must be stressed that the only child is far too often expected to live the life of a model child. Close scrutiny is focused on his behavior in isolation from the example of another child within the home. I remember describing to my mother the exploits of my classmates in the most vivid and explicit detail, hoping in vain that she would understand that the stories were primarily for her education, that other children misbehaved, did outrageous things, and spoke out brazenly without irreparable damage to themselves or to their elders. The danger of being only is being expected to be holy.

Furthermore, there are very common grounds on which parents and children regularly meet in unfriendly combat. When there is only one child, these battles tend to be magnified. In the multiple-child family, the adults quickly learn to stretch the perimeters of normal, acceptable behavior to take in the habits of their children, within the bounds of reason and good common sense. Therefore, the large family allows the development of individual styles of living through experimentation. It quickly becomes apparent to such a parent that the differences are essentially experimental in nature and occurrence and that the clean, neat, well-mannered child of today may turn out to be the disordered, rowdy, slightly rude youngster of tomorrow (or vice versa).

But the parents of the only child do not have examples of variable, experimental behavior immediately before their eyes to reassure them that ultimately, within a well-structured, well-adjusted home, all will right itself. Thus, their child's deviations from the normal in eating habits, cleanliness, neatness, manners, and the like may be viewed as catastrophes heralding malnutrition, disease, and degeneracy rather than as markers on the road to adulthood.

These deviations certainly require correction, and that is when the battles begin. The only child is no different from his peers; he, too, wants the privileges of experimentation and testing. A child is, without question, a child, whether he is the only one or one of a half dozen. The need to find his level, his personality, his self will lead him through many byways during his development. The only child must be permitted the same degree of freedom with the same reasonable restraints that any other youngster would be allowed—no more, no less.

AVOIDING UNHEALTHY DEPENDENCY

Because of the intense attention parents of an only child tend to focus on their youngster, he may tend to develop a dependency on the parent that is unhealthy. Parents may be overprotective, for instance, giving the child little opportunity to discover for himself the dangers and joys of his immediate environment. Most parents will differentiate between the hazards of a busy street and a quiet, wooded area well within viewing range. Unfortunately, parents of an only child are frequently unable to make these distinctions, viewing all experiences as potentially dangerous. All the child's adventures become cooperative missions led by carefully monitoring parents. With little chance for individual experimentation, the only child becomes increasingly dependent on his parents for each new experience. He relies on them to protect him from danger, to signal what choices he should make, to monitor his decisions. But growing up is the discovery that life is a continuing series of new experiences, and the only child must learn to cope successfully with the new and the unexpected all by himself.

One can fully understand the desire of parents to protect, surround, fortify their only child against outside failures and dangers. But the action cannot be condoned. The parents cannot live the child's life step by step. The child cannot be shielded from the daily experiences that constitute the learning process. Thus, parents must always be on the alert to prevent their youngster from becoming overly dependent on either of them. And if, upon analysis, it becomes evident that such a relationship has developed or is developing, the parent must very slowly ease the possessive hold upon the child, allowing for experimentation, encouraging sensible new adventures, mending small wounds and minor failures with the reassurance that the child will be better prepared the next time life offers another experience to be weighed, savored, and tested. Only with such experimentation, guidance, and counseling can a child learn to distinguish the possible from the impossible, the safe from the dangerous, the immediate from the future, the deserved success from the acceptable failure.

Occasionally, the parents become psychologically dependent on their only child. So much time, effort, thought, and caring have gone into the rearing that very slowly the fabric of the parents' lives slips away and is subtly replaced by the threads of the child's daily activities. Suddenly, the parents are totally immersed in the conversations, friendships, and future plans of their lone offspring. This situation is quite dangerous. They may begin by giving up some of their evening activities because no baby-sitter is quite good enough. Then, weekend activities gradually begin to be planned around the age-related delights of the child, and the parents' social and intellectual needs are quietly and definitely brushed aside. Vacation plans are primarily to suit the child and the adults find themselves visiting one carnival site after another. Life becomes a perpetual guided tour through Disneyland. Before too long, the child views his parents more as camp counselors than as parents and fully expects that his wishes will have first priority.

When the adolescent period begins, the only child tries to define his own personality. He must shed his parents' presence in order to test his freedom, and the sudden realization of the child's freedom and failure to reciprocate in what has developed into unilateral parental dependency can create the most painful, disruptive conflicts.

Like any other child, the only child must be made aware that his parents are special in their own right, with lives of their own, opinions that may differ, careers that may be disparate, and activities that are not always shared—in essence, individuals who are both independent and interdependent. If the only child is to feel comfortable about the ultimate need to separate from his parents in order to develop his own personality, this sense of parental independence and individuality is essential. The role model of parental individuality is thus of major consequence in a child's development. This individual independence of each member of the family is also a prerequisite for the parents' intellectual and social growth, self-esteem, and marital stability. And it is necessary if the parents are to win the ultimate respect and approval of their only child. How often I have been asked by only children whose parents have literally paralyzed their own growth in order to be totally accessible, "Doctor, when will they ever wise up? They're still living twenty years ago." Sadly, the only child is right; the parents have stunted their own lives through their misguided dependency on their child for stimulation and nourishment.

If you imagine a triangle, with both parents at the bottom and the only child at the peak, you can immediately see the problems of competition that can develop in the parents' relations with their child. After the parents place the child at that pinnacle, they may spend their days clambering up the sides, vying with each other for the youngster's attention. The child, in turn, soon realizes the extent of his power. He will begin to manipulate his parents, putting them into direct competition for his favor and affection. However, it is sometimes the parent whose distorted perceptions create the conflict. For example, a female only child's natural tendency to emulate her mother may assume unnaturally competitive qualities, as may her tendency to view her father as a source of strength and counsel in times of stress and pain. When misconstrued by overly competitive parents, these normal relationships assume abnormal form and are regarded as signs of advantage. The parents' normal roles may be distorted or even destroyed if competition for the child's affection and attention becomes a pattern. Furthermore, this situation is painful for the child, who comes to feel that he must constantly choose one parent over the other. How can a child be comfortable when he is judge and jury of his own affections, when the two people presenting their cases for his love are his own parents? Parents, particularly parents of an only child, must always remember that a child has the same vast, unlimited capacity to love that they themselves have. The child can love both parents deeply and meaningfully and can express that love in similar and disparate ways. Most of the only child's decision-making regarding the parental role models must be made on his own; he has no sibling with whom to compare notes.

Therefore, parents must begin to minimize competition and carefully and intelligently settle on specific roles and tasks early in their child's infancy. If parental role models are well presented and clearly stated, the only child will be able to give of himself to both adults rationally.

A case in point: Arriving for a house call one cold December evening, I was about to ring the doorbell, when the high-pitched voice of a five-year-old boy rang out through the closed front door: "Mommy, get me the comic book. Daddy, I want a Coke." As I stood there in the cold, listening, new commands were issued in rapid succession. Finally, I rang the bell. A frenzied, flushed father opened the door. He smiled wanly and directed me toward the bedroom of his only son, who was sitting up majestically in bed surrounded by a multi-tude of toys, comic books, packages of candy and food, and other temporarily discarded delights. The child viewed me with some suspicion despite our previous familiarity. Obvi-ously, I had intruded upon his castle.

After examination revealed that the little autocrat had nothing more than an easily treatable childhood infection, I guided the two parental serfs into the living room and launched into the first of a series of liberation talks. Here were two highly intelligent, thoughtful adults who had, in the span of five short years, allowed themselves to be totally dominated by their child. How could they have allowed such a thing to happen? According to them, the process of child domination had been subtle and unpredictable. It began with a sigh and a shrug. Why not give in this one time? He's the only one we have. Just this once. We have the time. We have the money. Certainly, we have the love. Just this once, even if he's asking for the slightly unreasonable. He's young; he'll learn. I'll wait until tomorrow, and then I'll put my foot down on this issue. I'll say no next week, next month, next year.

These are the attitudes that allow a child gradually to as-sume dominance over his parents. Only children are in a par-ticularly advantageous position to do this, and their parents are particularly vulnerable and susceptible. The child must have authority figures, people whose opinions, advice, com-mands and decisions he learns to respect early in his life. Without them, the child finds himself facing many problems alone, without the tangible support of strong advisors. Indeed, every child needs a "catcher in the rye," someone whose opinion can be respected and counted on in times of stress, danger, confusion, grief, and pain. A dominated parent is not that person. Therefore, both parents and child suffer a great loss when the child is allowed to assume control. The child has lost an advisor, a counselor, a guide; the parent has lost the pleasure of being mentor, teacher, and escort. So much lost; so little gained.

Parents must be on the alert for the danger signals. At their child's first attempts at control, they must gently but firmly establish themselves as parents and advisors, but as parents most of all, with the responsibility for final decisions on rules and regulations. As the only child experiences and learns, his respect for the function of parental authority will grow. Then, parental dominance can be lessened and more and more decision-making can be shared by the parents and their maturing child. But only from an established base of parent and child, mentor and pupil, can such a mutual friendship emerge. If the only child is king, he can hardly ever become the friend of his subjects, his too easily dominated parents.

Occasionally, the only child will fill a particular void within the life of one or both parents and will become a companion rather than a child. This, too, must be avoided at all costs. The sharing of adult concerns, the expectation of shared pleasures and equal responses, the mutuality of interests are all characteristics of adult friendships, not of parent-child relationships. Yet, the parent or parents of an only child will sometimes misinterpret the parent-child interaction to the degree that the youngster becomes a contemporary, rather than a child, an equal, rather than a charge, a confidential best friend, rather than a responsibility. This creates chaos in the developmental sequence of the child's life. He crashes prematurely into adulthood in a gasping effort to be the adult demanded by the parent-friend. Important growing periods are bypassed, only to be sorely missed in later life. Friendships are forsaken because they interfere with the tight pal relationship within the home. Development of the self is often sacrificed for development of the team, which consists of the misshapen parent-child comradeships.

The reverse situation may also occur. When bruised by the world that surrounds him, when rejected by the group or intimidated by his more sophisticated or worldly peers, the only child may sometimes attempt to readjust the parent-child relationship so that the adult is obliged to assume the role of childhood friend and playmate. Parents must resist this and encourage their child to make another foray into his peer society. This continued encouragement will eventually allow the only child to develop the same advantage that comes more easily to the sibling in the larger family: the ability to bounce back after peer rejection, anger, and hurt. This lesson is so important to the child's growth that the parent who permits himself to be his only child's surrogate friend, in times of need or on a permanent basis, is creating an adjustment problem that may bear bitter fruit in the child's adult lifetime.

AFFECTION AND THE ONLY CHILD

How much love can an adult expect from a child? And if that child is the only child, is the quantity of love available in inverse proportion to the number of accessible outstretched arms? The birth of the first child opens a whole new Pandora's box of love, very different from the intense affection the parents feel for each other. This new love is available for the parents alone, who are ready and more than willing to absorb vast quantities of demonstrable love from their firstborn. As more children are born, parental demands for love returned are easily satisfied by sheer numbers. But upon the head of the only child rests the often impossible responsibility for singlehandedly saturating the parents' needs for this reciprocal love.

Parents must remember that there are many stimuli which cause the young child to respond with surprise, excitement, and love and that all are somehow blended by the young, undifferentiating mind. A new toy, an animal, a friend, snow, a parent—all may receive the same quality of affection. To ask the very young child to make careful differentiations is unreasonable. Also unfair is the demand, either spoken or subtly implied, that the parents' needs for physical or verbal demonstrations of the child's love always be met to the degree that an adult may wish.

Each individual responds differently when asked to or moved to express such feelings. An only child may have deeply felt inner emotions, but they may rise to the surface and be mobilized into overt expression only sporadically. In spite of the singleness of the only child and the obvious need of parents for evidence of love returned, the quantity of the child's demonstrations of feeling must not be measured, only savored when offered, and then equaled by the parents in intensity and depth. Parents must resist the temptation to smother their one child with their intense feelings. If they do not exercise some restraint, the child who is unable to return such acts of affection in kind may feel guilt and self-doubt, and his parents may feel rejected. The key to the physical and emotional relations between the only child and his parents lies in the gradual understanding of the ways and means by which each best shows affection, respecting the similarities and differences in these forms of expression and allowing freedom (within reason) in the display and discussion of love.

The only child stands as the sole example of his parents' skill and capability. This is a very heavy burden and responsibility for the child to accept, and it must be minimized and de-emphasized. The only child is a full-time member of a *total* nuclear family. If the members teach, advise, counsel, cherish, and interact in many ways, the family unit will be its own monument to the wisdom, integrity, love, and freedom of the people involved.

3

Rebellion and the Only Child

ALL CHILDREN NEED To question the standards that have been set for them by their parents; they need to test these limits for themselves. Parents may be alarmed by these inevitable rebellions, but such behavior is a normal and significant part of growing up. If concerned parents thwart a mildly rebellious act, they do their offspring a great disservice because they have deprived him of the chance to learn from the experience. So relax. Most children will deviate from parental and societal norms just enough to satisfy their curiosity and come to their own conclusions. But there are some youngsters who need to break away more dramatically because they have been pushed by overprotecting parents, parents who have presented the youngster with a severely restricted world. This is frequently the case with the only child.

The single-child family tends to be tightly structured. The parents often set rigid rules and remain inflexible in dealing with the normal vagaries of youthful behavior. This is understandable because they lack the knowledge and the experience that come with raising more than one child. They have not learned how to be flexible without relinquishing their roles as guardians. Thus, it is easy for them to fall into the trap of stiff propriety. Yet the behavior of the only child, when he is at home, can be easily predicted and therefore monitored and controlled without too much physical and emotional effort (an attractive prospect for working parents). The parents, however, may still find the usual minor rebellions disturbing and difficult to deal with. So they should realize that the only child *must* rebel at some point—at least once, and probably much more than just once.

Rebellion does not necessarily mean that the only child is

dissatisfied with the way his parents are raising him; nor does it necessarily indicate that the relationship between the adults and the child has changed in any way. It simply means that the youngster has no brothers or sisters to observe and learn from so he must do all his own questioning and experimenting to find out who he is and where he is going. It is the responsibility of parents to adapt to their child's individuality, to understand the meaning of his rebellion, and to offer healthy, compassionate guidance. Rather then take a judgmental, punitive stance, they should provide their growing youngster with the firm support that he needs if he is to develop into a mature individual. Normally, the real danger with the only child is not the rebellion, but the passive conformity that the overprotective, dominating adults might seek to impose. Remember, you outnumber your lone youngster.

TYPICAL AREAS OF CHILDHOOD REBELLION

Eating Habits

One of the first areas that the infant or young child will use to test parental authority is eating. Attempts to regulate the infant's eating habits may result in subtle but exhausting battles of will. Here again flexibility is the best policy. Parents must control the feeding schedule, but in a rational, understanding manner. The schedule should contain sufficient leeway for the infant to be fed every three to five hours and should allow for variable consumption (by as much as four or five ounces) during a twenty-four-hour period. This will take into account biologically normal variations in the infant's hunger and still maintain a structured feeding schedule. The baby who cries to be fed every two hours will simply have to exercise his lungs until the next appropriate feeding time is reached.

Of course, parents must learn to adapt to the changing eating habits of their young child, but they must not allow him to use mealtime as the occasion for rebellion. Yet, even as he grows older, this is just what the only child will often try to do. The two- or three-year-old may refuse to eat the food that is put before him. (At this age, the child's caloric needs have diminished substantially from what they were during the earlier period of more rapid growth.) This total refusal to eat at mealtimes will usually be accompanied by excessive milk drinking or constant demands for cookies and other special treats between meals. This period of decreased food need (physiologic anorexia) is not in itself abnormal, but excessive consumption of milk is a medical problem because milk contains insufficient iron. If the child does not also eat iron-containing foods, he will develop a significant iron deficiency anemia. A child who eats too many treats may be establishing a pattern of obesity problems in later life because he will simply acquire excessive numbers of fat cells during these early years. Parents cannot demand that their only child eat what they serve, and they cannot force-feed him. But they *can* limit milk, desserts, and between-meal snacks. In this way, normal biologic hunger will ultimately bring an end to eating rebellions, and the child will learn that personal motivation (hunger), rather than parental demands, make rational eating habits necessary. It is vital that parents remember never to set the opposite example in any area in which they are instructing their child. The parents whose eating habits are capricious, excessive, or faddistic cannot expect their rebelling child to appreciate the need to conform to a sensible eating regimen.

Deliberate Disobedience

The toddler will purposefully stick a finger in a forbidden electric socket, drift toward the curb of a busy street, or run gleefully away from his mother. These are all minor rebellions. Only (and first) children may commit such acts more frequently and with greater earnestness because they are reacting to the somewhat oppressive focus of parental attention on them during this period of exploring and testing of their environment. The parents should be prepared for this behavior, set appropriate limits, explain the consequences of such disobedience, and follow through with consistent discipline. Although the rebellious act may appear harmless to the toddler, it may in fact have dangerous or even life-threatening consequences. But a sense of proportion is essential here. Not all behavior is life threatening. The parent who uses "don't" to apply to everything, from running out into a busy street to climbing on the arm of the sofa, will weaken and distort the significant difference between the minor benign act and the major dangerous one. A child who hears the same response for all forms of disruptive behavior learns to ignore all parental responses. The parent must decide what the priority items are and must then stick to the letter of the law on these, while remaining flexible in response to less serious rebellious acts.

Saying "No"

Between the ages of two and four, rebellion takes a very simple form: the word *no*. This must be viewed as a normal developmental period, a time of seriously examining the powers of the individual. Again, parents must decide in advance what areas of behavior, respect, and obedience are most important and what areas might permit leeway on their part and some decision-making on the child's part.

School

Once he has begun school, the only child has a number of opportunities to rebel, and to assert his developing individuality. Because education assumes particular importance to the family of the only child, the school milieu provides ripe territory for both small and major revolts. These may include school phobia, truancy, grades significantly lower than the child's recognized potential, or disruptive classroom behavior necessitating frequent conferences with teachers. Rebellion at the expense of education will have serious future consequences. Therefore, careful analysis is required to determine the reasons for the rebellion and the possible solution. It may sometimes be necessary to seek help from educators and medical personnel.

Another form of school-related rebellion involves educational goals. During my freshman year in college, I gave up all my premedical courses because I believed that I was pursuing a medical career to please my parents. But as the semester wore on, it dawned on me that the choice of a medical career was really my own. So, the next summer, I sat in hot classrooms without a grumble, making up the science courses that I had missed. The rebellion had had its price, but the ultimate decision to continue had been mine. The ability to rebel, to discard preconceived ideas, to view my life and myself with a fresh perspective was well worth the subsequent cost.

Friends, Activities, and Lessons

Not infrequently, parents will unconsciously but systematically select a circle of acceptable friends for their only child. They will expose their youngster to activities that they would like him to become interested in and arrange for lessons to develop his creative abilities. Much to their amazement and chagrin, the child will suddenly rebel by making choices diametrically opposed to those made by his parents. He will select friends from neighborhoods, religions, or social groups different from those preferred by his parents. He will stop taking the lessons or become so disinterested that the teacher will encourage him to discontinue them. This form of rebellion is common in the pre-adolescent period, when the child is searching for an individual identity. In the process, time may be lost for the talented pianist, excellent athletic abilities may not be fully developed, and friendships obviously doomed may be begun. However, this period of rebellion must be endured by the parents. They must remain available to their only child as advisors, but only when the child requests their guidance.

SPECIAL FORMS OF REBELLION

The only child has special ways to rebel against his intensely involved parents, usually knowing in advance what the full impact of his actions will be. The child may dramatically announce that he is about to run away from home, for example. The hurt and distressed parents blame themselves and each other, and the household is thrown into an uproar. The best tactic in this situation is to respond calmly and reasonably.

When she was two, our daughter Lee (at that time our only child), upset because we had refused to grant her a particular request, announced that she was leaving home. My wife and I quietly went into our room, took out a large suitcase, carried it silently into her room, filled it with her clothes, and carried it to the front door. Lee watched with widening eyes and gaping mouth. She followed us into the living room and stood there stunned as we placed the suitcase by the door. Finally, she spoke. "Should I go?" she asked in a plaintive voice. My wife maintained a serene, serious expression. "Only if you want to," she answered, adding, "I think we've packed everything." My daughter continued to stare at the fully packed suitcase, the culmination of her rebellious testing. Finally, she sighed and said in a very small voice, "Oh, well, maybe I better wait until tomorrow. I think it's going to rain." She then slowly and laboriously dragged the heavy suitcase back to her room, where she proceeded to unpack it and discard running away as a form of rebellion.

The only child may also attempt to hurt his parents with words. The child will try to punish the parent who has punished him or denied a request, by declaring: "I don't love you." All too often, the parents of the only child are devastated by that remark and may allow the child to see how upset they are. Such a reaction is inappropriate. The proper response is to state simply: "I understand that there are times when you are angry with us and don't love us. We feel that way at times, too. But it passes. We love you soon again, and I am sure that you will love us again." This should be said in a serious but understanding and gentle tone that will quell the rebellion and put the child's remark in the proper perspective. When handled in this way, the incident will teach the child a great deal about the complexity and variability of human relationships and feelings.

DANGEROUS TYPES OF REBELLION

Overt antisocial acts directed against others by the rebelling only child are a serious matter. Such actions must be dealt with firmly, with just and appropriate discipline. After the act itself has been dealt with, the parents can take the time to analyze the causes for the unacceptable form of rebellion. To delve into the whys before handling the immediate social and legal situation is to reverse rational child-rearing priorities.

Another form of rebellion that could have serious consequences for the child in later life is protracted withdrawal, literally cutting off parents, family, and the world in general. The child is punishing others by his absence. Most likely the world will miss the only child very little, but his parents may be devastated by his seclusion and rejection of them. If parents permit the recurrent use of this punitive withdrawal behavior, they are allowing a dangerous precedent to be established, for the child may resort to using it in response to social difficulties outside the home. However, what may seem to the youngster an easy form of coping is really a form of not coping at all. Consequently, long periods of silence, withdrawal, and rejection must not be tolerated by parents. The family is a communicative society, a microcosm of the larger society. Parents should make it clear to their youngster that no matter how upset, how angry, or how rebellious he may feel, the lines of communication must be kept open. This is one of the basic rules in every family, and it is especially important for the family with one child.

REBELLION AGAINST THE ABSENCE OF RULES

Occasionally, parents will be decidedly reluctant to establish firm rules and regulations. Perhaps they may be overly concerned that their only child loves them for being caring and compassionate people; consequently, they find setting limits and administering discipline almost totally impossible. Or they believe that discipline may have an adverse effect in the development of personality and therefore wish to do as little as possible to inhibit their only child. They want the youngster to experience the world in bountiful gulps, not fully realizing that the child may choke on life's opportunities because he does not also have appropriate portions of parental guidance. Or there may be conflict within the family concerning the importance of specific rules. This situation often involves unnecessary interference by grandparents and other relatives. Ultimately, the child will realize that there are no set rules, no forms of behavior that will be consistently acceptable. But whatever the reasons for the parents' unwillingness or inability to set guidelines, the child will feel stranded in a world that expects far more of him than his parents do. He searches for the figures of strength and consistency in his life, but they are missing. Insecure and anxious, the child may attempt to force his parents to give him the structure needed in his life by rebelling. Very often, the parents will not understand the meaning of the rebellion and will dismiss it as a phase. They may assume that school will straighten him out. But such an assumption is a serious mistake. Undisciplined behavior, failure to respond to authority, and overt or tacit disrespect will characterize the child's first school days. It would be unfair to expect such a child to behave in any other way because this is the only kind of behavior he has learned. This child is testing: testing his environment for the perimeters of acceptable behavior, testing his teacher in order to compare this new person's tolerance level and limit-setting abilities with those of his parents. He is looking for a model, an adult willing to point out the rules to which he must adhere.

It is also unfair to expect the teacher to play the role of surrogate parent, gradually introducing the child to the meaning of limits while attempting to teach and control a roomful of other children. But it is not unfair to expect the parents of an only child to provide the basic discipline that will enable the child to adapt to the demands of school. Thus, if the only child rebels outside the home, particularly in school, his parents should analyze their own disciplinary efforts. Preventive parenting is the key here. Do not squelch rebellion against firmly set rules and limits within the home. Allow the child to learn the risks and the consequences of transgressions at home. Then he will be ready to use this information as a guide to the world outside his home, where expectations are more complex.

Controlled rebellion monitored by understanding, perceptive parents is essential to their child's eventual emergence as an adult. Minor rebellions against authority must be viewed as natural, normal steps in maturation. But rebellion must be summarily rejected when it creates potentially harmful situations for the child, the parents, or others either at that moment or in later life. Rebellion should be a corridor of life through which the child passes on his way to maturity; it should never be permitted to become a way of life.

4

The Onliness of the Only Child

No MATTER How FULL the day of the only child has been, stuffed with laughter and companionship of small friends, sharing, comparing, fighting, there comes a moment when the world of other children ebbs away from the only child, when friends return to the privacy of their own homes. Then, the only child is alone in a world that has not been designed for the impulsiveness, the vagaries, and the experiments of a child, a world more carefully programmed and structured, a world of defense mechanisms and carefully considered conversation: the world of adults. At home, the only child is literally outnumbered: two adults to one child. Parents must take realistic steps to counteract this built-in imbalance, but this does not mean that they should try to emulate childlike behavior. Such an approach is foolish and irresponsible.

Children do not view the world in the same way that adults do. Events that are important to a child frequently have little significance to an adult. In a household where there is more than one child, peer-group adventures are carried home and shared with siblings; but the home of the only child does not provide that opportunity for sharing, offering instead only the sophisticated adult world of the parents. When an only child shares the events of his day with a parent, their significance often gets lost. The rationalizations or explanations offered by an intelligent, caring parent tend to diminish the excitement, the discovery of the moment.

Parents of an only child must be acutely aware of this difference in the way that they and their child perceive events, situations, and experiences. This awareness will enable them to be good listeners without also being solvers, advocates, or counselors. The continuity of the only child's peer-group relationships will not be completely disrupted by his isolation if his parents listen with genuine interest as their child reconstructs the day's events. And through the experience of retelling, the child will begin to learn to solve problems and make decisions on his own.

Parents and adult friends of only children, particularly young only children, often voice concern over somber or withdrawn behavior, silences, and dreamy absences. Therefore, it is important for them to remember that a child's priorities of excitement, joy, interest, absorption, and commitment differ significantly from their own. When several young children are together, they create their own world. Often, they will become absorbed in their own laughter, discoveries, and games that their behavior will disrupt the adult activities going on around them; then they will be reprimanded, sent from the room, or separated. But for the only child, this alternative to the adult world is not always available when he needs it. For the only child, there will be moments of intense joy or pain that cannot be shared because there will be no one he can turn to whose understanding and response will be in concert with his own.

EVENINGS

The *onliness* of the only child is often time-related: that is, there are specific times when the isolation of the only child may become intensified. Evening often finds the only child facing a companionless world. The young only child's heightened irritability during the hours before bedtime often expresses both a sense of absence of peer companionship and an attempt to force increased parent-child intimacy as a replacement. Understanding the cause of this regressive behavior will help parents find ways of stimulating their young only child and of interesting him in situations of independent play.

Parents can ease the isolation and boredom of evenings spent in a structured, demanding adult society. Wherever possible, company should include at least one other youngster of compatible age and temperament. If there are several other children present, the burden of forced friendship is avoided and the only child can choose his companions. If the parents have any control over the situation, they should give some thought in advance to whom the invited children will be. Their child may have expressed or demonstrated an antipathy to a specific child. An attempt to force these children to play together during an adult evening may prove as painful to the only child as having no young companion at all. If the selection is not the parents' prerogative and the other child is one with whom their child does not get along, they should attempt to make other plans for their only child, perhaps arranging for him to spend the evening with a friend or schoolmate. If no other child will be present at an adult function, or if the child's absence would be rude or inappropriate, the parents should bring sufficient diversions (toys, puzzles, games, books) to keep their youngster happily occupied and away from adult conversation. Another alternative is to arrange for the child to bring a friend for the entire evening or to be excused after an appropriate interval in order to visit with a friend. If parents do not demonstrate such consideration for the onliness of their child while he is young, the child may later strike back by refusing to attend family gatherings or adult parties.

Once the youngster has reached school age, he will often deal with the evening isolation period by becoming boisterous and interfering with parental conversations or activities, thus focusing attention on himself. The child may have unexpected and unwarranted difficulty with homework, and parents may spend many hours solving problems that they suspect the child is actually capable of dealing with alone. At this age, the only child is notorious for disappearing around dinnertime, playing outside longer than permitted, or staying at another child's home later than family dinner hours allow. Separation from his friends is often painful for the only child, and he may be reluctant to reenter the isolated world of his own home. Understanding these honest and emotionally significant reasons behind such abuses of family rules does not mean that parents should excuse the only child from the consequences of his behavior. Appropriate and consistent discipline must be meted out in this situation. A partial solution might be to encourage the only child to invite a playmate to dinner one or two evenings a week. An understanding about the time of the friend's departure should be carefully worked out in advance. In this way, the parents can tacitly demonstrate their willingness to help their child cope with the problem of onliness.

The older only child has a means of maintaining almost constant contact with his friends: the telephone. This is the

child's way of using a peer listener to bridge the empty parts
of his day; it may also reassure the insecure only child of his
place within the society of his peers. Parents of an only child
often complain that they get to use their phone very little because the child is continually on the line. Again, the only
child must learn that rules and family contracts apply to him
regardless of his onliness. Therefore, moderately flexible
phone regulations should be maintained so that both parents
and child have access to this important means of communication.

WEEKENDS

For an only child, the weekend can be a lonely time, an
arid stretch extending from Friday's last class to Monday's
first school bell. Saturdays and Sundays can be long and bar-
ren days for the only child if he has not formed strong neighborhood friendships. But this weekend loneliness can and
should be avoided. Parents of a young only child should plan
weekend visits to other families with small children. Weekend
play groups have proved quite successful in bringing only
children together, and because supervision of the group is
shared, this arrangement allows parents to have free time.
The experience can be very enlightening for parents. By
watching their young child play with other small children
(often other only children), they will see many aspects of the
child's behavior that they would not otherwise have the opportunity to observe.

The older only child's weekends require a different approach. The child should be encouraged to choose his own
activities. Because friendships are more significant at this age,
plans should be made for weekends spent with friends (either
at the only child's home or at the friend's). Very often in my
practice, I hear parents complain that their eleven- or
twelve-year-old only child "is hardly ever home. And then we
don't see her. She and her friend stay inside her room most
of the weekend. They do us the honor of coming to meals."
These parents, unfortunately, perceive the weekend extension
of peer relationships as competition, when in fact it is a normal way for the only child to fill the time until the next week
of group activity begins. Many parents of only children have
found that a satisfactory solution to the problem of the
child's weekend restlessness and their own needs is to spend

one day in shared activity with the child and to allow him to spend the other day with his friends.

SUMMERS AND HOLIDAYS

Summers can be devastating for the only child, particularly if most of his friends go away on vacation. But careful activity planning by parents will prevent the long, hot, empty summers experienced by so many only children. When parents of an only child select a summer vacation site, they should choose one where other families with children will be close by. This will give the youngster the opportunity to develop summertime friendships. Nothing is more disheartening for the only child than a sandy beach speckled with the immobile forms of adults, soaking up the sun's rays in silence. Parents of an older only child may want to make provision in their vacation budget for their child to invite a friend to join them for part of or all their vacation. If summer is to be spent at home, parents should investigate the various activities offered by their city or community. There are a surprising number of day camps, courses, play programs, creative workshops, and similar appealing activities available for children who remain in the urban or suburban environment during the summer months. (It might be noted here that, as a rule, only children are not the best campers. See Chapter 11, "Camp and the Only Child.")

How many parents can imagine the isolated feeling their only child experiences on Christmas morning when he opens his presents and comes upon the special one that he has been hoping for? The child can share his joy with his parents through an exuberant, thankful response. But with whom does he share the sudden excitement, the quickened heartbeat, the inner glow? How very well I remember Christmas mornings. I was bursting with the desire to share my gifts, my feelings, my excitement, my plans, but I was alone with a pair of admiring and happy adults who could not possibly have understood my exultation. So for me, Christmas morning soon became a period of waiting for my slightly older female cousin to arrive so that I could share the uniqueness of that special gift with her. One Christmas, I asked for permission to wait to open the gifts until she came. The look of hurt resignation on my parents' faces baffled me as much as my most unusual and somewhat insensitive request must have baffled them. The parents of an only child can deal with this splendidly if the extended family includes other children. They can arrange for holidays to be celebrations. A similar approach to birthdays (and other special occasions) is advisable. Gifts should be given to the child at a party so that he can share his immediate joy with other youngsters. The older only child might enjoy a birthday dinner to which one or two friends are invited; gifts can then be given to the child during dinner.

WHEN PARENTS ARE PREOCCUPIED OR TROUBLED

I received a phone call one Saturday morning; a small, tense, twelve-year-old voice asked me if I would stay in the office until her mother drove her over. She said very directly that she had to talk to me. I agreed, hung up, and waited. She arrived very quickly. Her face was taut; her lips were narrow and unmoving; she was near tears. She nodded to her mother, who silently disappeared down the hallway to the waiting room.

Debbie was the only child of middle-aged parents. She had had some very significant problems in adjusting to relationships with other youngsters, which I hoped were being resolved. She took a deep breath and spoke in a tremulous voice. "Thanks for waiting. You're the only one I can talk to." I remained silent, knowing that the words were being carefully weighed before I was permitted to hear them. She began again. "I have always looked to my parents for support when I needed them. And they were there. Now they're not there. And I feel so alone." She started to cry and pulled a tissue from her pocket. I leaned forward and frowned. "I don't understand. Why aren't they there?" She nodded. "My father's business is going badly. At least, he thinks so. And my mother is spending all her time at the business or sitting at home worrying. I can't reach her." "How hard have you tried?" I asked. She set her jaw firmly. "Hard. But nothing." We remained quiet for a moment. Then I spoke. "And you feel alone?" She nodded wordlessly, dabbed at her eyes, and then whispered, "Of course I do. Who else do I have?"

This is a serious and common problem faced by only children during times of parental stress or illness. Parents may become very self-involved, retreating into a protective shell that excludes much of the outside world, even their child. They may be so preoccupied with immediate problems that they are unaware of the subtle removal of emotional support from the child. When this occurs in a family with several children, the siblings will usually band together, the oldest often assuming a leadership role, until the stressful situation abates and the parents can assume their roles once again. But in the single-child family, the sudden withdrawal of one or both parents because of emotional, physical, or situational stress will result in a severe sense of isolation for many only children. This is particularly difficult for the younger child, who is less likely to have established strong friendships or ties with other family members or to have gained sufficient self-confidence to cope with such a crisis alone. When Debbie asked, "Who else do I have?" she showed insight and honesty. Her peer relationships had just begun to develop into meaningful friendships, but she was desperately afraid of jeopardizing them with the burden of her dependency and her family's problems. She had no other family in the city. And she had not yet achieved the full self-awareness that would have enabled her to withstand this sudden removal of parental support.

The parents of an only child must be acutely aware that because of the lack of surrogates within the home, removal of emotional support (no matter how subtle that support may actually be) can magnify the isolation and onliness of the only child to a pathological degree.

Obviously, what Debbie wanted was for me to have a talk with her parents and inform them in a subtle but honest way of her sense of aloneness and her feelings of inadequacy in handling her situation. I spoke to her mother that day and to her father the following week. They were both surprised and relieved to know what was behind their only daughter's apparent inner turmoil. As we analyzed the situation, it became clear that they had not included Debbie in any of their discussions of their financial problems. They had not asked for her thoughts or allowed her to help. Now they decided to try a total family approach to their financial crisis, and the result was that their only child found a source of personal strength and family unity in contributing to its resolution. Debbie became an active participant in the struggle, assuming substantial responsibility for household duties while her parents attempted to save the family business. She was no longer left out, no longer alone.

ONLINESS AND PERSONALITY

The singularity, the onliness, of the only child tends to result in certain characteristics that can be found in a high percent of only children. The child may exhibit marked independence or extreme dependence. Marked independence is occasionally exaggerated in the only child. The needs to shun authority figures, to assume leadership, to dominate conversations and activities all stem from the strong need to control all aspects of a situation. This pronounced need for dominant authority probably comes from a deep inner insecurity about what may result if control is lost. Extreme dependency usually results when parents treat their only child like a helpless creature, virtually living the child's life for him. Dependency problems are aggravated by the onliness of the child and by the lack of a sibling bond to counter-balance parental overinvolvement.

Because he has been reared alone in an adult world, the only child is very often extremely anxious to please others, especially parents and other adults. He may also be socially inept because of his limited experience with peer-group relationships. Therefore, the only child often exhibits the aggressive behavior of the individual trying too hard for peer-group acceptance. Self-aggrandizement and self-praise dominate the surface of the only child's behavior, but certainly not the core. Attempts at social adaptation may be extreme. The only child may assume affectations of behavior, voice, or dress in order to be recognized and gain acceptance, and these very things may produce exactly the opposite results.

The only child has a tendency toward oneness throughout his life. Oneness, withdrawal, and avoidance behavior are all very closely allied in the personality of many only children. Consequently, if this singleness is permitted to become a life-style, withdrawal from complexities and frustrations will become far too easy for the only child.

When the singularity of the only child is taken for granted, ignored, or abused by thoughtless, overprotective, overseductive parents, there will be trouble. Any child will behave like the worst sort of only child if he is targeted by parents or family for oneness. However, if the dangers of onliness are recognized, understood, and dealt with intelligently by concerned parents, it may ultimately prove to be an asset to successful self-realization, rather than an obstacle.

5

The Fantasy World of the Only Child

THE NORMAL CHILD BETWEEN the ages of two and four tends to be a rather solitary individual. If left in a room with other children and opportunities for various individual and group activities, the three-year-old child will often choose the singular activity. Although at this age all children display a normal tendency for isolation and internalization, the child from a multiple-child family is often forced by the very nature of the family structure to communicate and participate with older and younger siblings. Therefore, the ability of such a child to gravitate toward or even initiate group activity at the age of two, three, or four is far more developed than that of the only child. The only child is accustomed to a world in which there are no other children competing, struggling for recognition, interrupting, arguing, sharing, and playing in groups. Therefore, the only child is less well prepared to discard his shell of solitariness and participate in group play.

All children have fantasies, just as adults do. But children are not forced to deal with reality as directly and forcefully on a daily basis as adults are; therefore, they can daydream with greater ease and abandon. During this early period (between two and four), children have a natural tendency to create a fantasy world. With most children who have brothers or sisters, this fantasy world is transitory, swept away by the swirling activity of the other children and tolerated only minimally by the busy parents and by the older, more sophisticated siblings, who have conveniently forgotten their own fantasies. But the only child is not surrounded by the kind of concentrated human activity that would compete with his fantasies. In addition, the only child has a very strong reason

35

for creating and maintaining an imaginative life within his real daily life: the lower level of response within his immediate surroundings. All through our lives, we deal with difficulties by thinking through each problem and its possible solutions very carefully and then consciously or subconsciously trying these thoughts out on someone else before taking final action. Siblings often provoke arguments with the express purpose of testing out a method or a maneuver on each other. How often siblings ask each other, "What do you think they'll do to me if I . . . ?" By observing an older or even a younger sibling's responses to such testing behavior, a child learns to modify and shape his behavior in the future. Thus, direct or indirect sibling response becomes an integral part of a child's education in coping methods during early childhood.

All too often, the two-to-four-year-old only child, who is still quite solitary and just beginning to edge his way toward group activity, does not have the varied and changing group reactions of peers to use as a guide for the development of future behavior. There are no other youngsters for him to observe, on whom he can test responses and try out mannerisms, against whom he can measure intellectual growth and program small rebellions. To fill this gap, the only child will often create an imaginary sibling or friend. In essence, the fantasy world of the only child creates a mirror image from which the child is able to soak up the strength of his own reflection and reinforce and reaffirm his decisions before putting them into action.

THE FANTASY FRIEND

The fantasy creation may take many forms, but the most usual is the imaginary friend, with a name and a full physical description. The child will not share this friend with parents or other relatives and will often keep its existence a secret, fearing that an adult's rational response would deprive him of the friend. Parents report frantically that they often hear their only child talking incessantly to himself at bedtime, when he is alone, or just after an upsetting or exciting incident has occurred. When confronted with questions about an imaginary friend, the child may refuse to admit to the friend's experience or he may lie, claiming that an actual person was in the room but has "disappeared" or "run away."

It is essential for the parents of an only (or first) child to understand that the fantasy friend is more than a mirror before which the child adjusts and modifies his own behavior; this phantom friend is also exactly that—a friend, a companion. Fantasy is often the primary escape from loneliness for the only child, who is trapped for hours in an unintentionally unresponsive adult world. This phantom friend allows the only child to express thoughts, angers, joys, sorrows, feelings of inadequacy, superiority, and jealousy—all the basic emotions that everyone must learn to express and to deal with. The only child may feel uncomfortable and even unsafe in sharing these basic emotions with his parents or other members of the judgmental, sophisticated, and seemingly adapted adult world. It is often inappropriate for these childhood explosions of emotion to become part of normal parent-child interaction; these are experimental acts and confidences to be shared and experienced by peers. The imaginary friend allows the only child to express these emotions and gradually modify and absorb them into their proper context. Furthermore, parents cannot be constantly available to their child as an emotional sounding board. They must not feel guilty because their child has created a fantasy companion with whom he shares his experimental feelings and thoughts. The development of the imaginary friend is not necessarily a sign that parents have been inadequate or misguided. To view the phenomenon in that way and to force the child to deny his fantasy friend would be dangerous. Such a step would accomplish nothing and would create a serious conflict over what is in most cases a normal, healthy stage in the child's development.

The fantasy friend may not take the typical human form. It may be a composite drawn from favorite books, poems, or television shows. It may take the form of an animal, usually a dog or a cat. These imaginary pets tend to be small, furry, cuddly, nonprotective, and loving animals to which a small child can easily relate.

My oldest daughter, Lee, had a fantasy friend for many months during her second and third years. She created this fantasy friend at a time when all the adults in her world had become extremely preoccupied with their own problems. Her father was being taken out of residency training unwillingly and shipped overseas by the armed forces; her mother was unexpectedly pregnant and not feeling very well; her grandparents were upset by the impending separation from their children and grandchild. Lee needed a friend with whom she could communicate, share, and tolerate the surrounding foolishness and confusion. Just before the army's announcement had created such upheaval, Lee and I had spent an afternoon sharing the joy of Disney's *Pinocchio*. She had insisted that I buy the book and read and reread each chapter to her daily. With each reading, she connected herself more completely with the threads of the story until she had woven her imaginary friend, Jiminy Cricket, out of the experience. Jiminy stayed with us for many months. Lee conversed quietly with him in corners of rooms. She laughed with him, chided him, occasionally fought with him, all within the privacy of her inner life, shutting out the sudden and disturbing lack of adult control she saw around her. I even suspected that the small space in her bed next to the wall was reserved for her tiny friend. My wife and I knew of Jiminy (Lee had admitted to his existence), but we seldom talked about him. He was *her* friend, and she in no way wished to share him. He crossed the Atlantic Ocean intact, obviously less worn and frazzled than my wife and I and more adaptable than his friend, my daughter. He remained with Lee for several more months.

In the meantime, a baby sister, Karen, had entered the household, and it soon became apparent that a conflict was brewing in Lee's mind. As her younger sister grew and became more responsive, several serious dilemmas were being thrashed out by the maturing older sister. Did she still need her imaginary friend now that a real friend had arrived? Outside the home, her circle of friends was widening, and she was beginning to participate in group play. Where did Jiminy Cricket fit? If he were to stay, should he be shared with her younger sister or still coveted by Lee alone? As might be expected, after several quiet and reflective weeks, Jiminy Cricket silently and permanently left our home. He was not mourned by his friend. He had been faithful, useful, and important, but he had been outgrown. None of our three other children developed imaginary companions; they had each other. But Jiminy taught Lee and her father many lessons beyond those to be found in *Pinocchio*.

Our experience with Lee's fantasy friend had one disturbing element that I have since encountered many times in my practice. She often blamed her imaginary friend for actions and misdemeanors that she herself had committed. Being the first and thus the only child at the time, she was constantly seeking approval from the adult world around her. This adult world was her world, there were few peers to approve of or reinforce her activities. Consequently, she feared the disapproval of her parents with a heightened intensity, and she used her imaginary friend to divert their attention from her negative behavior. In this way, she had dangerously and seriously mixed up fantasy and reality, and we, as parents, had to deny both the existence of the fantasy friend in the context of our world and the possibility that the misdemeanor could have been committed by anyone but Lee herself. The existence of the imaginary friend seemed to stimulate her desire for experimentation and discovery, almost as if she felt protected and reinforced by the fantasy experience. This growing exploration of the world around her was healthy, but her failure to accept responsibilty when experiments resulted in antisocial or unacceptable behavior could not be condoned.

At special times (e.g., during and immediately after periods of punishment, discipline, or denial), the only child has a natural tendency to withdraw into solitary play and contemplation. Parents often find this exasperating, but it is important for them to realize that this is not totally abnormal behavior for the only child; it is a way of dealing with life's stresses and frustrations. My advice to the parent of the child who retreats into a highly private world at such times is to be patient and then to reinforce the reality of the situation. The child must be allowed time to work through his shame, embarrassment, and anger at the disciplinary action or word his behavior has necessitated. After the child has dealt with the consequences of his act and has made personal decisions, the parents may approach him and reassess the reality of what happened and what can be done to prevent such mutual discomfort in the future. The parent who attempts to deal with the child's retreat mechanism at this time only diverts attention from the crucial issue. The act and its consequences *must* be understood. This is a cornerstone of personality formation.

Only children seem to need a pronounced amount of physical expression of belonging and affection. Frequently, they form prolonged attachments to inanimate objects. Teddy bears, pandas, other stuffed animals, and dolls are held, nursed, nurtured, loved, and carried everywhere in a manner that may confound and confuse the parent. Like the imaginary companion, this inanimate object receives the attention ordinarily reserved for a sibling or friend and represents a kind of surrogate peer relationship that is separate from the child's relationship with his parents. Again, like the fantasy friend, this inanimate object allows for reaction, reflection, and reinforcement, even though the response is the child's own. And like the imaginary friend, the inanimate object often receives not only abundant affection but also the full brunt of the child's anger. The only child uses it as a whipping boy because he is unable to act out his feelings of hostility toward the adult world.

Michael was a blond, blue-eyed, freckled three-year-old who greeted me with a heart-melting grin when I sat on the edge of his bed to examine him for his high fever. He was at that time an only child. Both parents were medical professionals. Propped up on the pillow next to Michael was a worn, brown teddy bear with a ragged, threadbare black nose, two button eyes (recently sewn back in place), and a missing right ear. After my examination revealed little more than a transient viral infection, I began to chat with the disarming young boy. I picked up the teddy bear and frowned. "He's worse off than you, Mike. What happened to his ear?" Michael reached out and took the bear, hugging it to his chest as he very seriously answered, "I had to pull it off. He was very bad to me, and I got mad at him, and I pulled it off and threw it down the toilet." I was surprised to hear this angelic-looking boy recount such violent treatment of his favorite toy so seriously and self-righteously. I shook my head and asked what the bear had done to warrant such an action. Michael proceeded to describe in detail a punishment that had been meted out to him for having knowingly disobeyed his parents. He went into great detail about the anger and shame he had felt at the discipline, but he transferred most of the anger and hostility to his teddy bear, as if the punishment had come from the stuffed animal rather than from his parents. He finished by commenting, "And I was so mad, I pulled off his ear. I was a little sorry. But maybe he won't do that to me again." Michael had acted out his anger against the stuffed animal because there was no other outlet available for him at the time.

IMAGINARY SIBLINGS AND OTHER FANTASIES

Sometimes the only child will populate his fantasy world

with imaginary siblings. Because of the intense parental concentration on the only child, he may feel the pressure of high expectations and constant surveillance. The creation of imaginary siblings is a rather desperate attempt to achieve a more balanced nuclear family. When the only child creates an imaginary sibling rather than an imaginary friend or pet, the parents should thoroughly and sensitively examine their relationship with their child. How much freedom does the child have? Are they being overprotective? Do their expectations exceed their child's capabilities? The imaginary sibling is a clear signal that the only child is extremely uncomfortable with his onliness and wants a sibling to absorb some of the intense attention that his parents have lavished on him.

Conflicts between the only child and his parents may lead the child to fantasize that he has been adopted and therefore is unloved. Such dramatic self-pity is not at all uncommon as a child explores and establishes his place in the nuclear family. Most children at some point in their very young lives fantasize that their parents are not their real parents. (Frequently, this is a response to deserved and honestly administered discipline or to imagined rejection.) For the child who has brothers or sisters, this fantasy quickly vanishes in the face of daily realities. But the only child has no siblings who look like him, no older siblings who remember mother's pregnancy or his birth. Consequently, the fantasy may persist, particularly in reaction to the highly concentrated attention the child receives, which may generate considerable resentment in the child. The persistence of the only child's fantasy that he is adopted is an important signal to the parents that they may well be traveling the wrong road in rearing their youngster.

COPING WITH THE CHILD'S FANTASIES

How should parents handle their only (or first) child's fantasies? What are the danger signals that normal childhood fantasy has deteriorated and become psychologically unhealthy? In essence, how do you learn to live with Jiminy Cricket?

Parents of a child who has created an imaginary friend must clearly indicate that they are aware that the friend exists, that they are not alarmed or threatened by it, and that they understand the importance of this companion. However, at no time must they allow the fantasy friend to become part of their own or the family's reality. The imaginary friend must remain part of the child's internal world. At no time should the parents acknowledge their acceptance of the imaginary friend as a real or viable creature independent of the child's fantasy. The parents must never use the imaginary friend to make a point, get the child to perform a task, or administer a warning or punishment. To do so would not only reinforce the fantasy and distort reality but would also prove very threatening and frightening to the child. I remember the parents who pulled up an additional chair to the dinner table specifically for their only child's imaginary friend and soon thereafter consulted me about the sudden decline in their child's appetite. A child does not have the sophistication to cope with the mixing of fantasy and reality within the supportive, external world he shares with his parents; he can deal with fantasy only in the context of the inner world that he himself controls.

The use of fantasy friends and pets often indicates that the child has insufficient peer contacts. A child who creates a fantasy pet may do well with a real pet. But the parents must also pay more attention to current family concerns and priorities. Family stresses may have added to the only child's sense of isolation, and the fantasy friend should prompt a new investigation of the family members' relationships.

Parents must attempt to create and maintain the proper balance between reality and fantasy in their child's life. When the child shows signs of significant withdrawal into a world of fantasy and does not respond to the stimulations of reality, parents should take several actions. First, they should assess the child's day for stimulation and contact with other children. Second, they should examine their relationship with their child in terms of expectations, expression of affection, both physical and emotional. Third, they should look at tensions that may exist within the home (marital, financial, family.) Fourth, they must slowly and gradually reintroduce the child into peer activities. If the child still remains locked within the world of fantasy and struggles against the introduction of reality, the parents should consult a pediatrician or child psychiatrist.

Few children allow their fantasies to take over their lives. When very young, they use their fantasies to help them mold their responses and ultimately their identities. At first, only children may have only their fantasy friends with whom to communicate. But as the child begins to adapt to group activities (a process that often takes longer with the only child) and to develop one or two friendships, the fantasy friend no longer has a purpose in the child's life.

6

Peers and Friends of
the Only Child

A CHILD WHO GROWS up with brothers and sisters faces new confrontations, tests of position and strength, and compromises every day. Each incident must be solved between the young contestants or reported to the parents. Questions of ownership must be settled; new rules must be established. These negotiations often begin before speech and certainly before organized thinking. They are the first lessons in peer relationships for the youngster, and they prepare him for encounters with other children outside the home.

The only child does not have this preparation for the peer relationships that lie ahead. For the most part, the only child negotiates with the adult world, where the contracts are quite different, the expectations more clearly defined and less variable, and the responses more predictable and less flexible. Therefore, the training that the only child brings to the arena of peer relationships may well prove counterproductive to successful acceptance into group activities.

When a two-year-old child pulls a book from the hands of a four-year-old sibling, the reaction is immediate. The older sibling grabs the book back. If this has happened before, or if the book has been damaged, the older child may strike the younger child or in some other way indicate that repetition of the act will receive an intensified reprisal. The young child quickly learns that it is important to respect the rights and possessions of others.

But what happens when the two-year-old only child wrests a book from the hands of a parent? Usually, the parent will calmly take the book back and explain to the child that such an action is not permissible. Next, the parent may outline (in terms poorly understood by the child) the punishment the child will receive if the action is repeated. The response is slow and primarily verbal. (In fact, the child may fail to understand this lesson and may instead view the taking of the book as an effective way of getting attention.) Clearly, the only child will have a distorted picture of what he will find beyond the door of his protected, adult-oriented home unless he is taught the realities of peer relationships.

INTRODUCING THE ONLY CHILD TO PEER-GROUP ACTIVITIES

The formation of peer relationships and friendships is an essential part of mature, socially adaptive behavior. But the only child often finds it difficult to make and keep friends. The only child is usually very slow to leave the normal period of isolated play. Nevertheless, between the ages of three and five, he should be introduced to comfortable, congenial group activities. Parents should see to it that this is accomplished sensitively and without making the child self-conscious. The four-year-old only child is likely to be puzzled by a group of laughing youngsters at play. Although he will probably want to join them, he may not know how to begin. Without help, he may remain on the edge of the group for much of his childhood. (Indeed, some only children remain on the outside of social activity for most of their lives.) Therefore, parents must be prepared to give the child as much encouragement as he needs to overcome his initial fears of group situations.

However, it is vital that parents allow their only child to experience for himself both the successes and the failures inherent in peer relationships. He has to learn to resolve problems with peers by himself; his parents cannot live his life for him. This lesson must be learned as early as possible. The proper role of parents at this stage is supportive but still peripheral. They should listen to both the child's joys and his sorrows without passing judgment or giving unsolicited advice.

Because he has been somewhat isolated from other youngsters in his earliest years, the only child may experience more than the usual number of difficulties in social situations. Parents should deal impartially with strained peer relationships. In mediating disputes, they must be fully aware that their child may be in the wrong. It is a serious error for parents of an only child to accept the child's grievances against other youngsters without question. They should investigate all sides of an argument, and if their child is wrong, they should help him to realize this. Otherwise, a pattern of recurrent disruptive behavior and fighting may be established.

The only child is frequently faced with the necessity of participating in group activities such as parties, classroom games, school outings, and team sports. Unless he has been properly prepared by his parents for the demands of group interaction and has accepted that both success and failure in peer relationships are to be expected, and unless he has learned to solve his problems by himself, he may react to peer activities in ways that can cause him serious trouble and unhappiness. For example, he may select another youngster in the group as a model, emulate that child's behavior, and lose all individuality in his effort to win acceptance. Or he may try to hide his insecurity by attempting to dominate the group. The common result is rejection by the group. Still another unhealthy reaction is avoidance. The child may choose solitary play or the company of adults because he fears rejection by his peers. Some only children will attempt to conceal their anxiety by adopting a veneer of adult sophistication in dealing with other youngsters. Such inappropriate behavior will be scorned by the members of the group. Parents and teachers must be alert to such reactions and must deal with them realistically and with compassion. The child must be helped to understand the anxiety, the fear, and the suspicion underlying his behavior and to make a happier adjustment to the group experience.

LEARNING TO SHARE

Within the world of his immediate family, the only child generally has had little need to share. His toys have been unequivocally his; he has selected the games he has played. But the peer world demands sharing, and sharing is a difficult concept for a three- or four-year-old to grasp if he has never been faced with the prospect. Parents can help their only child to understand the benefits to be gained by relinquishing individual possession and control: acceptance by the group and inclusion in group play.

But it is important to be very careful with the only child. He may misunderstand the true meaning and function of sharing in peer relationships. Because of the difficulty he generally has in forming relationships with other youngsters, he may attempt to buy his way into the peer group. The only child must realize that sharing is not unilateral giving in or giving up. Sharing means receiving as well as giving.

Sol was fourteen years old when his parents told me that they were concerned because their son had no friends. The young man willingly discussed this problem with me. As an only child, he had been somewhat slow socially. He had bought his way into a group of neighborhood youngsters by bringing out new toys for them each day. If he was unable to produce a new plaything on a particular day, he accepted the group's condemnation. As he grew older, he equated friendship with giving without receiving. By the time he was in his early teens, he deeply resented the lack of response from the youngsters whom he believed were his friends. They never called him; he always had to call them. He invited them to his parties; they rarely invited him to theirs.

He had every reason to be disillusioned, but the problem was essentially one of his own making because he had failed to understand a basic rule of friendship. Sol had created these relationships himself. He had selected his friends on the basis of their response to his giving rather than their willingness to share with him. But friendships that do not include sharing are sham friendships. He was unconsciously setting himself up to be hurt by the demands and lack of response of his unappreciative companions. As he explored his distorted view of sharing, he was able to understand why he was so lonely and unhappy. He realized that he had to learn a new way of selecting potential friends and of negotiating friendships.

My only subsequent contact with Sol was in the lobby of a movie theater several years later. He looked happy and more mature. He rushed over to shake my hand, and we chatted for a few minutes. Then he smiled and, indicating two young men waiting near the box office, said he had to return to his friends. It was clear that he had learned to form friendships in which he received as much as he gave.

DOMINEERING

Because the only child often becomes the center of attention in his family, he may attempt to become the center of his peer group's attention as well. This often leads the only child to try to control and manipulate the group's activities.

Unfortunately, this tendency toward dominant behavior will severely limit the child's acceptance by other youngsters. Children select their leaders depending on the type of activity to be undertaken and the immediate needs and talents of the individuals in the group. Such shifting is essential to the successful functioning of any group of young children. The child who seeks to dominate all the group's activities may find instead that he is rejected by the group because he is unwilling to accept a more flexible role.

This effort to dominate may be the insecure only child's way of handling a group situation that he finds threatening. When he enters a peer group and finds himself unfamiliar with the rules, he may seek to control the group in order to protect himself. The group will rarely tolerate such behavior and will eventually reject him. Because he has not previously experienced rejection in response to his domineering behavior within the home, he will find rejection by his playmates inexplicable and frustrating.

The permissive, adoring parents of an only child may be quite tolerant of their little tyrant, who rules the household with his temper tantrums. They may assume that he will outgrow his dominant behavior. But they are wrong. The little tyrant will grow up to be a big tyrant, and his domineering behavior will bring him pain and rejection. No group of peers (whether they are young children, teenagers, or adults) will tolerate the sulky, tyrannical only child who demands constant attention and complete control over people and situations.

Attempts to dominate must be stopped early, and prevention must begin at home. The child must never be allowed to control or dominate his parents. Therefore, parents should be alert to any emergence of domineering behavior. When they detect it, they must take immediate steps to administer discipline, assert authority, and clarify family roles. If this can be accomplished (and sustained) within the home while the child is very young, the chances that he will try to dominate his peers will be greatly diminished.

Domineering behavior that springs from insecurity and fear of the group can be prevented if parents introduce the child to group play as early as possible. Although children under four may play together only sporadically, the presence of several other children in the play area will help the only child to learn the rules of group play by association. And he will be more comfortable when he is faced with the necessity of full group participation.

SINGLE FRIENDSHIPS

Most only children find the introduction into group play traumatic and, at times, painful. Some will persevere and learn the language and tactics of the group. These children will blend gradually and comfortably into the group. But most only children find the effort too arduous and the wait for acceptance too embarrassing and demeaning. Thus, the only child is rarely a group person. More often, the child will very carefully select a single friend. He will wait until he finds another youngster who possesses observable characteristics that suggest a preference for single friendship. Usually, the other child has many of the same fears of group relationships and therefore chooses single friendship out of the same necessity. Not infrequently, both youngsters are only children.

These singular friendships are usually quite intense. The friend may become more important to the only child than his parents. Although this may puzzle and hurt the parents they must understand that the formation of a friendship is of the greatest importance to the only child and cannot be taken for granted. Furthermore, the parent-child relationship generally is quite comfortable and secure at this stage and needs little reinforcement. It is unwise for parents to view these intense single friendships as threatening, unnatural, or too confining socially. They should under no circumstances attempt to expand the only child's circle of friends without considering the feelings and wishes of the child. (This dictum does not apply, however, if the chosen friend is behaviorally unacceptable to a major degree.) The child will correctly view such action as interference of the most damaging kind. He will fight desperately to maintain the friendship and will resist being forced into a group.

For some only children, the period of single friendships may be replaced by definite entry into group activity as they mature and gain confidence. However, other only children will never become group people. They will continue to be essentially single-friendship individuals, maintaining a number of acquaintances and establishing a few intense friendships. Yet these youngsters will normally grow into mature, healthy adults as long as the single friendships are allowed to flower without parental interference.

The greatest hazard of the single friendship is the loss of the friend. When this happens, the child experiences an exquisite sense of rejection and abject loneliness. There are many reasons why a friendship ends. The other child may move to another town, or the two youngsters may fight and refuse to be reconciled. Manipulation by unintentionally cruel parents may divide the children. Other activities may intervene constantly so that the friendship deteriorates from neglect. Or the friendship may gradually weaken as the interests of the two maturing children pull them in opposite directions. The only child may try desperately to adapt to the friend's new life-style or interest, but eventually the gulf between the two will become insurmountable.

The parents of an only child can be very helpful to their youngster during that painful times by providing the warmth and comfort that will enable the child to overcome his loss. Brief periods of isolated play may follow the loss of a friend. But these will diminish if the parents gradually and gently urge the child into situations where there are other children. This is not to suggest that parents force their only child, recently estranged from a close friend, into unwanted group play. Parents must understand that the loss of a close friend may make the only child more hesitant and more fearful of subsequent rejection. But they should encourage him to be open to the possibility of new friendships. In this way, sensitive parents can help their grieving child to explore new relationships slowly and gradually. When the only child displays interest in a new youngster, the parent must wait and watch patiently, no matter how much they want this new relationship to work. The children must be allowed to negotiate the friendship on their own terms.

IDEALIZED FRIENDSHIPS

The friendships of the only child tend to have the quality of idealized sibling relationships. Whereas the child who has brothers or sisters is intensely aware of the faults of the other children in the family, the only child does not have the reality of these relationships to guide him in friendships. Only children tend to set the same high standards for their friends that they set for themselves. They expect model behavior from their companions. In effect, they expect their friends to have all the qualities desired in an ideal brother or sister. These unrealistic expectations can undermine a friendship and doom it to failure. Unless the child learns to have more realistic expectations of others, he may be condemned to a life of failed friendships.

Parents can be very helpful in this regard. The youngster must learn not to judge a friend too severely; he must learn to accept the friend's faults as well as his virtues. Parents can set an example by displaying tolerance of a friend's failings. The parents who agree with their only child's unrealistic standards will simply reinforce a concept of friendship that no one can live up to.

COMPETITIVENESS

The only child tends to be highly competitive. This, too, can lead to difficulties in the child's friendships. The friend of the only child often finds himself in an impossible situation. If the only child views a friendship as some kind of contest, he creates a situation in which his friend can neither win nor lose without losing the friendship. If the friend wins, he threatens the only child; if he loses, he loses the respect of the only child. Consequently, the only child often finds it extremely difficult to maintain intense and enriching relationships over an extended period of time. He may go through his life without fully understanding why his friendships deteriorate and why the patterns are so consistently repeated. Therefore, it is vitally important for the parents of an only child to de-emphasize their youngster's competitive nature and teach him that the essence of friendship has nothing to do with winning or losing.

FRIENDSHIPS WITH OLDER PEOPLE

Only children have a fascinating tendency to develop warm friendships with elderly people. These relationships may spring up between the child and a grandparent, a neighbor, an aunt or uncle, or any other individual who shows an interest in the youngster's daily activities. Often, the only child will sit for hours and listen to the older individual's reminiscences. At other times, the only child will talk to the older person as he might talk to a brother or sister, testing ideas, sharing problems, expressing anger. The child feels quite comfortable with the elderly friend, who offers him experience without judgment, advice without expectations, warmth without possessiveness. The quiet wisdom of age blends well with the lonely search for values that troubles so many only children. The loyalty that develops between the two is likely to be deep and lasting.

RECURRING INSECURITY IN LATER LIFE

The insecurity and awkwardness that overwhelm the unprepared only child when he faces a group of his peers for the first time may recur throughout his life. It may require great effort for the older only child to approach a new group and seek acceptance. All the old anxieties may return when a new group encounter proves difficult or unrewarding.

By the time I was ready to attend college, I felt that I had overcome my typical only child's difficulties in dealing with group relationships and activities. But during the first semester of my freshman year, I experienced an unexpected group rejection. The fraternity I wanted very much to join decided that I must wait for admittance. Suddenly, all the past group denials and the old fears of rejection rushed back into my consciousness. For several uncomfortable weeks, I relived the painful sense of onliness that had plagued my childhood. Thanks to an understanding father, I was quickly able to overcome the flood of unhappy memories that threatened to overwhelm me. He advised me to be patient and to remember all the positive group experiences of the past. The following semester, I was invited to join the fraternity of my choice. My first impulse was to reject the offer. If the group could reject me, why couldn't I reject the group? Again, my wise father helped me to gain the proper perspective. He reminded me of the need to accept and forgive, a need that only children are often unprepared to acknowledge in the face of their anger and disillusionment at rejection.

7

The Early Maturity vs. the Prolonged Immaturity of the Only Child

EVERY CHILD MATURES AT his own rate. This rate is influenced by the child's environment, the life demands, the number of older people in his life, and the joy and pain that he has experienced. An additional element is involved in determining the rate at which an only child will mature: his onliness. It is not uncommon for the only child to stand out among his peers as being either prematurely mature, outwardly worldly, and grown-up or markedly immature, dependent, and unusually amorphous in personality.

There is a tendency for the only child to take one of these directions. But these detours can be avoided. The principles of preventive parenting are essential in this situation. Parents of the only child must be on the alert for the influences that move the child away from the normal path of maturation. In this way, they will guide their child in the direction of full emotional maturity.

EARLY MATURITY

Mindy's father was a college professor; her mother was completing a doctorate in speech pathology. Because of their productive, burgeoning careers, they had decided to have only one child. Each parent communicated daily with young adults on a highly intellectual plane, arguing professional points and dealing with youthful behavior in the authoritative manner characteristic of the classroom situation. Unfortunately, they brought this behavior home with them to their relationship with their growing daughter. Dinner conversations were intense intellectual exercises in which Mindy was encouraged to participate. Indeed, if she did not interject a comment or two, she remained essentially unheard because her childish stories and recollections had no place in the context of her parents' conversations. They discouraged frivolity and strongly encouraged serious thinking in both overt and subtle ways. Mindy was taken to reasonably adult films and theater very early in her life. She was included in dinner parties and encouraged to mingle, which essentially meant that she had to become a well-behaved, attentive listener and to attempt with all her tenuous emotional strength to withstand temptations to giggle, laugh, shout, run about, or simply slip away to find other youngsters with whom she could share more appropriate and pleasurable conversations and games. Gradually, Mindy began to adapt; she learned the skills and language and artful defenses that allowed her to blend into and be accepted by the adult world of her parents. By the time she was eight, Mindy was going on thirty-eight.

But she had lost something essential along the way: the ability to be a child. Spontaneity and flexibility had drifted from her grasp. She never learned the necessary behavior patterns that would have enabled her to play and establish successful relationships with other youngsters. Between the ages of eight and eleven, Mindy found herself being gradually excluded from the peer groups in her neighborhood and her school. Then, her two very close friends began to drift away. They found that they had few things to say to her and even fewer things to share with her. Mindy was unable to understand some of the unsophisticated, unstructured joys and problems that were the basis of the other children's conversations; they, in turn, were perplexed by her seemingly haughty and cynical approach to simple, everyday childhood pleasures.

By the age of eleven, Mindy no longer had a peer group into which she could retreat; she was alone in an adult world. In fact, she had been so well programmed that she did not want to retreat. Instead, she wanted to be included in her parents' complete social calendar, and she became furious and unmanageable if she was not. Because she had been conditioned to consider their life also hers, she interpreted any failure on the part of her parents to include her in their activities as an overt rejection. It was not loneliness but rebellion and despair that brought Mindy to my office.

It is important that parents of an only child understand what happened to Mindy. Such an understanding will enable them to spare their own child an unfortunate premature adulthood. Very early in her life, Mindy was thrown into a race (the world of adults) for which she had had no training and no skills. The other runners were older, more experienced, knew the course, the dangers, and the detours. A person so handicapped will naturally try harder, run faster, push, strive, and adapt so as to at least remain in the race. And so, Mindy ran.

But unless trained for the adult marathon slowly and carefully, the maturing child who tries to keep up will become a superficial runner, perhaps keeping pace, but never finding out why he is running, where he is going, or even who he really is.

Language, for example, can cause serious difficulties. Adults have their own language, complete with its own phrases and its own slang. They use inflections and anecdotes to make or illustrate a specific point. The only child who is trying to keep up with the adult world must learn this language both to maintain contact and to be able to understand the rules of the adult game. But the language created and used by children is very different. If the only child cannot speak this special language, he will use the only language he knows: the sophisticated language of adults. And he will find himself mocked and shunned by other youngsters who do not understand the language, although they may recognize it as a part of the adult world.

Adults are creatures of mannerisms, many developed to fit previous situations, many copied from highly regarded friends or family members. Children are relatively free of such behavior. They spontaneously choose the physical, mental, and verbal responses that fit the situation at hand. They are delightfully and at times exasperatingly unpredictable. In contrast, the only child who is allowed or encouraged to become a participant in the daily life of the adult world to the exclusion of the world of his peers will rapidly select styles and patterns to emulate. The models he picks will be those that to his young, unschooled mind are most attractive or compelling or dynamic. Consequently, he will not only develop set patterns of behavior long before he is sufficiently mature to do so intelligently but will also often select those patterns of behavior and role models least spontaneous and flexible and least socially acceptable and adaptable. When this occurs, the only child will find himself lost in the world of his peers because his attitudes and responses are unacceptable to them. The other youngsters will move away from rather than toward this adult actor masquerading in child's clothes. Because of his adult mannerisms and attitudes, the only child will find himself ultimately rejected by his friends and his own age group. He will then most likely retreat more completely into the role of adult, no matter how ill-fitting and uncomfortable it is, because he believes it to be acceptable and safe.

Parents must avoid this dangerous situation at all costs. They should encourage peer relationships and discourage the regular inclusion of their child in adult gatherings. They should express pleased acceptance of their only child's young friends and games, and they should demonstrate their interest through discussions of the child's peer activities. In essence, they must view their only child, not as an extension of themselves, but as a growing, maturing individual who is still in the formative period of his life. The only child must be allowed to make the ultimate decisions about when he will begin to move into the adult world, to what degree he will involve himself in it, and how much of his previous world he will leave behind him or carry along as he matures.

PROLONGED IMMATURITY

Andy's parents had quietly but effectively shielded him from all possible problems during his young life. All decisions were made for him; his life was structured and protected. He had had some difficulty making friends, spending most of his free time (including vacations) with his parents. He was lonely, but his parents assured him that time would take care of his problems. When he entered high school, Andy made a special effort and succeeded in cultivating friendships with two boys who were in his class. When these two boys decided to go away to a New England camp that summer as counselors-in-training, Andy decided to join them. Although he was afraid to leave home, he was even more afraid that he might lose his friends if he stayed behind.

His confused and worried parents overwhelmed him with

advice about what to do should he experience a whole catalog of problems, each of which they described carefully and vividly. At camp, Andy found that his immediate supervisor was an autocratic counselor. The young boys in his group quickly sensed Andy's discomfort, fear, and growing homesickness. The counselor constantly reprimanded him, and the boys taunted and teased him. He tried to cope and sought advice from his friends, but they could offer only their friendship and support. Andy soon realized that he would have to solve the problem himself, but because he had never learned to cope, his defenses crumbled quickly. He began avoiding his supervisor. He neglected his tasks, taking long, self-pitying walks through the woods. He tried desperately not to call home, knowing what he would hear and fearing what his response would be. But finally he could not make the simplest decision without being reduced to trembling anxiety. He called his parents, who told him to come home immediately.

When he told the camp director and his counselor that he was leaving, they were surprised; they encouraged him to stay and try to resolve his problems. His friends were sympathetic, but Andy correctly detected a note of disappointment in their encouragement. He returned to his home, where he was received with open arms, words of reassurance, and consoling explanations about his failure to adapt.

However, Andy continued to be anxious and withdrawn. He had seen all too clearly his inability to cope with stress and failure, and he had suffered a serious blow to his self-esteem. He was ashamed and embarrassed. In addition, as he told me in consultation, he had realized that the facile explanations offered by his parents placing the blame for his failures on others were both inappropriate and inaccurate. He told me that he felt adrift, unable to rely on the advice of his parents, whom he felt had not been honest or realistic with him. He recognized that he lacked the inner resources to deal with his problems. He despaired over the possible loss of his friends, who meant a great deal to him. Furthermore, he was afraid that he would repeat the same behavior each time he was faced with a new and uncertain situation. I reassured him that he had already come a great distance in realizing the crux of his problem. But building his confidence in himself as a functioning, independent person required both a great deal of hard work on his part and absolute cooperation from his parents.

Conferences with Andy's parents were difficult, and progress was slow. It was extremely difficult for these well-meaning parents to realize the necessity of altering their approach to their only son. They began by reluctantly allowing Andy to make his own decisions concerning such matters as who his friends would be, how he would spend his allowance, how much time he would devote to homework, when he would go to bed, and how he would spend his weekends. All these rather basic responsibilities were the necessary beginnings for this young man in his effort to develop confidence in his decision-making abilities. His parents gradually accepted the fact that Andy had to make his own mistakes, that they could no longer protect him from the pitfalls of living. Andy was encouraged to test himself slowly and carefully, using his friends rather than his parents as role models. He came to realize that he could not always succeed and that he must learn from failure. He was urged to explore each new situation carefully for his role in the ultimate outcome, regardless of success or failure.

This campaign eventually helped Andy to discover his capabilities, his strengths and weaknesses, his needs and resources. Very gradually, his parents permitted him to move away from them emotionally. As he demonstrated a growing inner strength and increasing involvement with others, his friends accepted him back into their circle. He began to make his own decisions and live with the consequences. Several years later, Andy was able to go to a college hundreds of miles from home, where he succeeded in adapting to a new environment and new people and in coping with his initial isolation and normal homesickness and with increased study demands. He is now a senior, happy, successful, and independent. He remains very close to his doting but now more realistic parents, yet he is no longer dominated or even overly influenced by them.

It is a sad fact that not all such only children realize their imprisonment within their family in time to repair the damage and grow into well-adjusted, independent young adults. Many remain overly dependent, unable to move in the direction of emotional maturity.

Why would loving, well-meaning parents consciously or unconsciously attempt to prevent their only child from becoming a mature, independent individual? Growing up means growing away. The child's ability to think for himself means that he may honestly disagree with his parents, that he will no longer accept their ideas unquestioningly. These developments can be extremely threatening and exquisitely frightening to overly involved parents. They fear the loss of their influence and, ultimately, the loss of their child.

How do such parents block their child's emotional growth? They vividly describe the dangers of any impending action, any new experience. They make it clear to the child that they are concerned about his ability to make decisions, to cope with the outside world, to become a self-reliant human being. Their constant warnings fill the child with anxiety. The one thing that this child does not hear is any expression of faith in his ability to take control of his own life.

The child learns to view the outside world as threatening and full of potential catastrophes. And, indeed, the world is full of dangers for this child because he is totally unprepared and therefore totally vulnerable. Then, when he experiences disappointment and failure (as he inevitably will), his fears are confirmed. He is, as he has been warned, unable to cope with life, and he hurries back to the protection of his family. He will be more hesitant to venture out into the world again because he fears that failure is unavoidable. But all of us fail at one time or another. Learning how to recover is an essential part of growing up. The only child who is shielded from failure will be unable to learn these important lessons, and as each year passes, he will become increasingly frightened and dependent. Parents *must* allow their only child to learn that failure is an acceptable part of everyday living.

By suggesting (no matter how subtly) to their child that he is incapable of reaching the top of the ladder of maturity, parents only succeed in making the climb dizzying and terrifying. The frightened child will cling to the lower rungs and beg his parents for constant assistance and reassurance. Such only children are maturational cripples, maimed by well-meaning parents in the name of protection. This child's love for his parents quickly turns to resentment and distrust. In seeking to win their child's love by shielding him from life's inevitable hurts and dangers, they will achieve the opposite: the loss of that love.

8

Education
and the Only Child

EDUCATIONAL ACHIEVEMENT Is generally very high on the list
of priorities in the family of an only child. The parents of
only children tend to be well educated themselves, and they
are likely to want their children to match or to surpass their
own accomplishments. And even if it is not often spoken of,
the child understands that education is the mark of success in
the world around him.

Parents who have more than one child grow used to the
normal variations in intellectual ability among their children.
But parents of an only child often find it difficult to evaluate
their youngster's potential realistically. Consequently, they
may aim too high and set standards far above anything the
child can hope to attain. These standards are set very early in
the child's life, and the youngster accepts them as the norm.
Any achievement that does not meet this high level of expectation is viewed by parents and child as a failure. The only
child who labors under the burden of overestimated potential
faces daily frustration.

CONSEQUENCES OF HIGH STANDARDS AND
UNREALISTIC EXPECTATIONS

A significant proportion of school phobias, unexplained
failures, drop-outs, and outstanding students who suddenly
cave in emotionally are only children. And, in fact, the response of most only children to high parental expectations is
extreme: either they become compulsive overachievers, or
they slowly, quietly give up completely.

Adult approval is extraordinarily important to the only
child. If the child correctly perceives the value his parents

60

place on educational achievement, he will drive himself relentlessly in order to win that much-needed approval. He will strive to attain the highest possible level of success in school; he will literally overachieve. This compulsive behavior pattern has inherent dangers, not the least of which is the fact that at some point in his life, the only child will face a task that exceeds his abilities. But his habit of overachievement will not allow him to recognize and accept this, and the inevitable failure can be devastating. The overachieving only child often falls apart in the face of teacher criticism, poor grades, or the loss of an award to a classmate. But the occasional inability to perform a task is not an all-consuming disaster. Life, after all, is fraught with disappointments and failures. The only child must understand that failure is acceptable. He must learn to respond to it in a constructive way, maintaining a healthy, balanced perspective by viewing it in the context of his successes.

A period of very real danger for this child occurs during the college years. The young person will be faced with a greatly increased workload, and he may experience serious difficulty in maintaining his previous high level of achievement. To the overachieving only child, an average academic performance in college may be equal to failure.

The opposite reaction is retreat from the educational arena. If the child realizes that he will never be able to meet his parents' expectations, he may stop trying. He may make an attempt to discuss his problem or he may engage in sporadic episodes of disruptive behavior in school. If these signals of panic and building depression over underachievement go unrecognized, the youngster will begin to withdraw. He will apparently lose motivation, lapsing into inattentive, irresponsible behavior and even truancy. Unless parents realize that they are expecting far too much of this only child, he is likely to end up achieving far less than his true potential.

It is therefore imperative that parents appraise their only child's abilities and inabilities realistically. They should attempt to keep their natural and understandable parental ambitions from distorting this evaluation. The only child must be allowed to proceed and to achieve at the rate that is best for him. In essence, the only child must be allowed to be his own person.

Bernie had worked extraordinarily hard within the limited, protected environment of small private schools and a warm,

supportive home. While he was in high school, he studied late
into the night and gave up much of his social life on weekends in order to complete work that other youngsters had
been able to finish in much less time. He could easily have
been an average student, but he realized that his parents
would have viewed this as a failure. Pleasing his parents was
so important to Bernie that he had never stopped long
enough during his successful high school career to ask
whether he was pleasing himself. In accordance with his
parents' fierce desire that he go to a "good" school, he entered a prestigious college. It soon became apparent to him
that he was not going to match his previous achievements. In
the highly competitive intellectual environment of this Ivy
League college, he could be no more than average at best—
and only after a great deal of work and the continued sacri-
fice of his social life. In addition, his chances for admission to
the professional school so carefully planned for by his parents
were diminishing as each day of his freshman year passed.
He tried to explain his concern to his parents. Their response
was to advise him to "work harder." They assured him that
he would soon adapt to his new surroundings. At no time was
he able to make his caring, intelligent, but insensitive parents
understand his situation. He tried his very best, but at the end
of his first semester, Bernie's grades were average or lower.
His parents were hurt and confused. Why had he let them
down? Couldn't he try harder? All would not be lost if he
would just get down to hard work.

But by this time, all *was* lost. Bernie had overachieved for
so long that he could not push himself any higher or harder.
In the third week of his second semester, he dropped out of
college, stayed in the city where he had been going to school,
and got a job in a department store. His parents were devastated. During the Christmas holidays, Bernie came to see me.
He was not happy in the department store. Although he had
always accepted his parents' goals as the right ones for him,
he knew now that he could not attain what was expected of
him. He admitted that he could and would try to set and to
meet more realistic career goals if that would satisfy his
parents. Bernie had not yet realized that his first responsibility
was to satisfy himself. But, then, most only children are late
to arrive at this realization. After considerable discussion with
his parents, Bernie entered a state college and went on to the
successful, if not outstanding, completion of his degree. He

became a teacher, continued to attend school, and completed graduate degrees. Bernie's story is not unique. He represents an army of only children who have been expected to achieve a level of success that exceeds their abilities. Unlike Bernie, many of these young people have not realized that alternatives *are* available to them which allow them to lead stimulating, satisfying, and productive lives.

PREPARING FOR THE FIRST DAY OF SCHOOL

The parents of an only child may not fully realize the difficulty and pain of the separation that occurs when the child begins school until the day arrives. It can be a nightmare of crying, scuffling, running away, complaining of a sore throat or some other ailment, and any other device the child can think of to delay or prevent the separation. For this reason, it is important that the child be exposed to a school-like experience as early as possible. The earlier the exposure, the better the eventual adaptation. A nursery school or play group can be extremely helpful in preparing the child for that traumatic first day *if* his mother is not always present. The child must experience *both* the group activities and the separation from his mother if the preparation is to be successful.

A prearranged visit to the school the child will attend, including a meeting with the principal and the teacher, can be very reassuring to the youngster. The parents' attitude is all-important: they should express enthusiasm about the school experience when shopping with the child for school supplies and clothing; parents should project an attitude of excited anticipation over the fine new adventure of school.

A few years ago, I served as preceptor to a young hospital resident who was working in a well-baby clinic. A woman had brought her only child, a five-year-old boy, to the clinic for his preschool physical. (It was spring; the child was to begin school in the fall.) The mother had the greatest difficulty coaxing the child to let go of her hand long enough for the doctor to examine him, but the gentleness and warmth of the physician helped to ease the child's anxiety. Throughout the examination, the young boy turned often to make certain that his mother was very close by. When the examination was completed, I asked, "Are you expecting difficulty getting Thomas to go to school in September?" The woman nodded and said, "Yes. I can't even leave him to go to the store. I take him everywhere. I don't know what I'm going to do when school begins. I know he won't want to go. He'll cry. He won't want to leave me." I looked at the boy. He was absorbing every word. Without realizing it, this devoted mother was preparing her youngster for a classic case of school phobia. The boy was being taught to fear and hate school and to indulge in disruptive behavior once he got there.

Over a period of months, the resident and I began to help this mother loosen the overly tight bond between herself and her only son. We advised her to find appropriate neighborhood play groups for him and suggested that she and her husband begin going out in the evening and leaving the boy with a responsible baby-sitter. We discussed visiting the school before it closed for the summer and obtaining permission for the youngster to spend a half hour there without her. In addition, we located a day camp where the boy would spend two weeks during the summer. The purpose of all these suggestions was to make it possible for this only child to go to school without feeling that he was deserting his mother and without feeling that he must rebel in school to avoid disappointing her. Finally, we focused on the mother's problem. We explored satisfying and productive activities with her that she could turn to during the time the boy was in school.

ADJUSTING TO SCHOOL DISCIPLINE

There are two aspects of school that may involve special difficulties for the only child: its group activities, and its regimentation.

Because the only child is likely to be accustomed to solitary or single-friend activities, he may have some problems adapting to the classroom situation, in which he must interact with many other children. Now, he must learn to share books and other materials. But even more important, he must learn to share the attention of the teacher with other youngsters, waiting patiently for his turn to be heard. The child who has had an early introduction to peer-group activities through nursery school or play groups will be better prepared to cope with the new challenges of school. Parents should encourage their only child to participate in the many group activities that school has to offer. They may also find it helpful to invite one or two classmates home for an afternoon's play, gradually increasing the size of the group as the only child becomes comfortable in the company of more young friends.

Classrooms, even so-called open classrooms and kindergartens, have certain rules and regulations. If the child has been reared in a relatively permissive home environment, if rules have not been clearly stated and discipline has not been consistently administered, he may engage in confused and disruptive behavior during his first weeks and months in school.

The teacher is a very important person in the life of the only child, and it is not uncommon for the youngster to identify strongly with his teacher. An insecure parent may find it extremely difficult to cope with such competition. This parent will countermand the teacher's requests, belittle the teacher's comments, de-emphasize school, and thus seriously hamper the child's efforts to learn. A confused only child, torn between his loyalty to his parents and his desire to win the approval of this important new adult in his life, will become a worried and resistant nonlearner. Therefore, if the only child is to achieve success in school, any conflict between home and school must be eliminated. Teacher and parents must cooperate. The teacher must understand, remain patient, educate the parents and the child; the parents must begin to share their only child with the outside world. Such behavior is the child's way of testing the limits of the school's rules. It may be his way of seeking the guidance that the lax discipline of his home environment has failed to give him. But if the child's maladaptive behavior goes unchecked, he will not learn.

Teachers and parents must understand the causes of the child's actions. They can do a great deal to solve the problem by keeping each other informed of the child's adaptation problems. Parents and teacher must not argue over correct discipline, structure, or rules; they must work together to help the only child understand what is expected of him in each important area of his life. Parents must support rational school discipline and encourage the child to obey; at the same time, they must strengthen the disciplinary atmosphere at home in order to bring home and school into closer harmony in the area of behavioral expectations. School and home need not have identical standards, but they must not be so different that the only child has to make constant drastic adaptations in his behavior.

GOING AWAY TO COLLEGE

Parents and their only child should not minimize the difficulties they may experience when it is time for the young person to go away to college. Short vacations and summer camp have had definite beginnings and ends; both parents and child knew that they would soon be reunited. But going away to college is truly a turning point for the only child and his parents. It is a clear break in the family's life-style, and it can be frightening.

There are no older sisters and brothers who have been through the college experience to offer advice to the only child, to tell him what to expect and what will be expected of him, to serve as behavior models. The only child, a cultivator of singular rather than group friendships, is likely to travel light in the social sense, knowing the loneliness he will experience until he can form new single friendships. It is not unusual for the only child to go through periods of depression and loss of self-esteem and some consequent academic problems during his freshman year. Parents must expect these emotional and educational troubles and be ready to offer advice and support when their child turns to them. They must avoid showing alarm, reaffirm their faith in the young person's ability to cope with this new educational challenge, and calmly and forthrightly discuss the importance of a balance between scholastic and social activities.

When an only child goes off to college, his parents also face a challenging new adventure. It can be a difficult time for the couple if they have not anticipated the problems of this moment in their lives. The couple whose investment in their only child is the most significant, perhaps even the only, bond that they have shared will now be forced to face their relationship.

Both parents will have to cope with feelings that may not have emerged while the child was still at home. Both will have to seek out new activities to absorb the energies that they previously put into raising their child. Most important, they must make every effort to keep in constant communication, to grow together intellectually, to nourish their friendship. They must share much and yet maintain separate and distinct lives and identities. They must never allow their child to block their relationship; they must not become locked into the roles of mother and father. For the parents who have retained their separate identities and a strong commitment to their marriage, their child's departure for college will be, not an end, but the beginning of a period of growth.

Her only daughter had been away at college for three years. Mrs. G. had taken a part-time job and appeared to have adjusted to this separation from her child. Her husband was active in work with needy youngsters in their community. Yet, Mrs. G. was obviously very depressed. It was snowing; Mrs. G. stared blankly out my office window for a long time before speaking. "She's not coming home for Christmas. She didn't come home for Thanksgiving. I want to go out there, but Bill doesn't think we should." I nodded and said, "You must be disappointed." She began to cry, shaking her head. "You don't understand. Christmas has always been so important to the three of us. But she isn't coming home. Don't you see what that means? She doesn't need us anymore. Not at all." I leaned toward her and asked, "Do you feel that you've succeeded with Mary or that you've failed?" Her response was quick and tinged with anger. "What do you mean? Bill and I are very proud of Mary. I think we've done a damn good job." I nodded. "So do I. You must understand that when you've done a good job with your child, she'll become self-sufficient. Mary still needs you, but for very special times. She also knows that you don't need her, that you and Bill have your own lives. So she feels free to miss one holiday, knowing that it will not destroy the strong adult relationship between the three of you." She frowned and wiped her eyes. "Are you saying that the better the job you do as a parent, the less your child will need you when she grows up?" I nodded. "Yes. I am saying that." She took a deep breath. "Let me think about that."

As I later learned, Mary had accepted an invitation to spend Christmas with a friend but had decided to surprise her parents by coming home in time to celebrate New Year's Day with them. She stopped in to see me before she returned to school. I casually asked how her parents were doing. She smiled radiantly. "Perfect. Just perfect." We chatted for a few minutes, and the mature, happy only child left my office. I never heard from Mrs. G. again.

9

Creativity, Culture, and the Only Child

THE PARENTS OF AN ONLY child have limited themselves to one investment. From this singular investment must come many dividends, not the least of which is the realization of the child's creative potential. This creative force is one that must be unearthed and carefully shaped. Inevitably, the parent views himself as the dynamic impetus to the child's discovery and fulfillment of his own inherent creative possibilities. The parent, if untempered and ill-advised, may overload the wires of inner talent, creativity, and drive and, as a consequence, short circuit the only child into a passive, creatively unresponsive adult.

A very subtle negotiation is involved when a child enters into any outside activity under the parents' scrutiny. It deals exclusively with expectations and is usually unspoken, but the child learns that certain levels of attainment and accomplishment are expected of him by his parents and his teacher. The only child is often too eager to please all adults. Furthermore, the parents' expectations may exceed what can normally be achieved by the child at a particular stage in his development. Because the only child has no siblings against whom to compare achievement, he will accept the parents' well-intentioned but unrealistic high hopes as attainable goals and he will continually fail at his extracurricular activities. Despite the instructor's obvious pleasure or acceptance of the rate of the child's creative achievements, the child will be unable to accept the teacher's evaluation.

Obviously not every child can be outstanding. If we all were exceptional in these creative areas, the stages would be full of award-winning performers. We do not all possess exceptional abilities, but most of us can explore creative expression with great pleasure as amateurs. The child whose expectations are toward a goal of true excellence has a high possibility of failure, and is consequently vulnerable to a sense of failure as a person. He is also often too consumed with the success factor to enjoy the excitement and expansion of the creative experience. The parents of the only child must relax, construct realistic and rational expectations, and allow their child to experiment with his own creative abilities. Otherwise the potentially creative only child may face early failure which will cut him off from active enjoyment and cause him ultimately to turn off the truly expressive, creative aspects of his character.

The only child wants desperately to perform well, not only to please the teacher but also to please his parents and win continued approval from all concerned. In addition, the only child usually establishes personal goals that exceed the norm set for the child coming from a large family. These very high personal standards spur him to constant maximum efforts. Thus, if parents overload their only child with cultural and creative activities, they may create serious inner anxieties in the child which will manifest themselves in physical, emotional, or school problems.

"She can't get to sleep at night," Shirley's mother said, "so I can't wake her up in the morning. And then we fight and she cries. When I ask her at midnight what she's doing laying there staring at the ceiling, she always just says, 'I can't get to sleep.' " The child was waiting in the outer office. Her mother glanced nervously at my closed door. "There has to be something physically the matter. She's not even eating as well as she did before." I waited, then asked, "Before what?" The woman sighed. "Before this year. She was eight this year. Is this what happens when they become eight?"

I indicated that sleeplessness was not a normal eight-year-old problem and carefully questioned this mother about her child's past and current medical history. She was an only child of working parents and had managed rather well in childhood adaption and interpersonal relationships until the current crisis. Her health had been normal with the exception of one rather mild case of viral pneumonia at the age of six. Shirley's parents came from backgrounds that permitted only high school educations. Each went on to obtain college degrees during nights and summers, working during the days. Shirley's mother had taken only a six-month leave of absence to have this planned only child, carefully selecting a house-keeper and scheduling her at-home time so that she remained in control of Shirley's upbringing. Until this problem period, things had gone along quite successfully.

I saw Shirley alone. She was a petite, large-eyed, very seri-ous eight-year-old who spoke directly and without hesitation. When I asked her if she knew why she couldn't get to sleep at night, she smiled. "I think about what I'm going to do the next day in my classes." "School classes?" I asked. She shook her head, "No. Regular school is easy. I know what I'm going to do there. I think through what I'm going to do in my special classes." I learned that Shirley was also taking lessons in ballet, tap dancing, art, and drama. She looked seriously at me. "I'm very busy during the day," she said, "so I lay in bed at night and plan. Yesterday, my tap teacher told me I was the best in the class." I nodded and asked, very quietly, "When do you play with the girls and boys in the neighbor-hood?" She shrugged. "I don't have the time."

Shirley could not get to sleep because her life was so crammed that she had no time to unwind. She had selected the hours before falling asleep as time to simmer down, think through her priorities, make decisions. This prevented her from dropping off immediately to sleep and was the cause of the family concerns about her late sleep and waking prob-lems. Rearrangement of Shirley's and her family's priorities, decrease in the intensity of her extracurricular activities, and setting time aside for her to participate in outdoor play and for leveling off before bedtime gradually solved Shirley's sleep problem. She was still able to involve herself in many stimu-lating outside activities, but at a pace which was more realis-tic for a normal eight-year-old girl.

In order to fulfill his creative promise, a child must be given special training or education. This will require lessons. Two primary factors will deter the average parents from in-volving their children in a large number of creative activities at one time: money and transportation. Lessons and exposure to varied cultural experiences can be quite expensive. How-ever, when there is only one child upon whom to lavish all of the surrounding and available cultural wealth, particularly in cities, then the financial considerations are of less immediate significance. But children must still be taken *to* the activity; the days of the visiting piano teacher have long since passed. Thus the parent may find himself driving from special class to lesson to concert every day after school and all during the weekend.

One of the most creative gifts a parent can develop in his child is how to use free time. Few adults know how to structure their lives to allow the full spectrum of work, play, relaxation, and entertainment. The only child who lives and grows in this adult world observes the hurrying, the borrowed moments to relax and laugh, the postponed hours of contemplation and creativity. This child will emulate, and gradually accelerate, the pace of his life until it imitates that of the adult world around him. Days are spent in school; after-school hours are heavily scheduled with extracurricular lessons, weekends are often filled tagging along with parents on their rounds of visiting, partying, shopping. Nowhere in this schedule of creative education is found the lesson of how to use free time in a sensible and productive way. The child of the large family escapes often from the world of his parents and settles comfortably into an unstructured dimension where he can experience relaxation, rest, and pleasure without guilt. The only child does not have such an accessible peer world and depends on his parents for exposure to unstructured creativity. The parent must also teach him the positive and essential importance of balancing the hours of the day.

The only child may become involved in an excessive number of extracurricular lessons because of overly ambitious parents or his own unrealistic performance standards. He may be trading very valuable time from friendship-forming and sheer fun for isolated time spent developing individual skills. There must be a healthy and sensible balance. But most importantly, parents must remember that the only child, no matter how great his talent, must also move out into a world of people. The background training for this is of equal importance to individual creative success. Without it, the parent is shaping a lonely, isolated person.

QUALITY vs. QUANTITY

Parents frequently suffer a loss of objectivity when dealing with the creative possibilities of their only child. Parents may not be critical about the competence and quality of instruction offered to their child. In the creative arts, it is highly important that the training be of the best quality and taught in the proper sequence and pace. Bad habits on stage, with a musical instrument, paint brush, or ballet shoes are very difficult to break and repattern, even if the subsequent teachers are more professional and competent. Be wary of too much and be careful of the inferior. Give the only child the benefit of the most competent creative experience in the correct sequence, with the right social balance and at the right age.

A word of warning to the parents of the only child! Do not start your child at the creative task too early in his life. He will fail and become frustrated. It must be remembered that each child matures and develops at his own pace. Therefore, parents must observe and get to know their own child—his capabilities and limitations, his range of attention and concentration abilities, his physical dexterity. Waiting one or two years to begin piano lessons or dancing lessons will be of little importance to the active, dynamically involved only child.

TALENT AND INTEREST

One of the greatest problems surrounding the creative life of the child—in particular the only child—is that its prime force may come from the parents' own unfulfilled and unrealized ambitions or fantasies. The parent who yearned to be able to paint will insist upon art classes for the child, or the parent whose theatrical drives have been limited to local amateur productions will push his or her youngster into extensive drama classes. Pushing a child to the achievements which the parent has not realized is not exclusively the problem of the only child, but it is often intensified.

Decision-making and selection of specific activities all too often are made by the parents without consulting the child. Parents must recognize their integral role in the whole area of their child's creative future. That future will rest upon the eventual choices made by the child himself. Without the full and enthusiastic cooperation of the child, parents see the ultimate disintegration of the creative experience. Some children simply rebel, refuse to go to lessons, avoid practicing, or remain inattentive. Others diligently attend all of the lessons, practice, and take part in recitals or exhibitions. But then, when adolescent rebellion emerges, the creative experience is the most decisive activity to be discarded. The adolescent knows the impact of this response to the culturally ambitious parent. The time he has invested is insignificant next to this gesture against something over which he had little or no control in his younger years. Had the decision been his, the creative activity might have had real personal meaning and importance, and this rebellion would be unnecessary.

Karen danced well. She had been taking lessons since the age of nine and had moved quickly to the most advanced classes so that, by age fourteen, she was quite accomplished for her age. Her mother had been a dancer, as had her grandmother, who actually pursued a professional dancing career. Karen, an only child, moved readily from tap shoes to toe shoes, her progress watched closely by both mother and grandmother. In her image, they saw much of their own talent, now unused and remembered with fond regrets.

At fifteen, Karen announced that she was no longer going to dancing school, that she no longer cared about dancing, and, moreover, wanted no part of the family tradition. Cajolery, promises, bribes met with her firm refusal. When I gave her a physical examination for her summer job as camp counselor, her mother openly brought up Karen's dancing. The subject simply overflowed during her conversation. Karen glared angrily and simply stated that her mind was made up: dancing school was completely out of her future plans. It did not require much to learn that Karen was in the midst of an important attempt to develop her own identity. Discussion revealed that Karen realized she was fulfilling the wishes of her mother and grandmother, and not her own.

Karen could not be forced to dance. Her mother and grandmother allowed her the chance to experiment with other aspects of her social and cultural life. She went back to dancing school the following year and took several courses. Eventually, she dropped out. Despite her talent and potential, Karen obviously did not want to continue dancing. But she learned two things from her experience at dancing school: to carry herself with the poise of a dancer, and with the assurance of an independent person.

With so many expectations funneled into the only child, parents may overlook another essential factor in the decision-making process surrounding the child's creative future: what are the child's talents? What does the child do well? How tragic to see the clumsy child struggling in a dancing class, trying desperately to please the teacher and live up to the expectations of the parents. The very same child may suddenly come alive with a musical instrument or a paint brush or pencil. A child may reject an activity because failure is predetermined by clumsiness or shyness and replacement by another activity should be a joint parent-child decision with a realistic look at the reasons behind the choice. The most crucial area in the whole selection process of the child's creative outlets is what the child wants to do himself.

TRIPS AND VACATIONS

Part of the cultural environment is the trip—whether the short-distance, limited-time trip or the long-distance extended-time trip. Each has virtues and pitfalls.

Often the parents will schedule trips to museums and places of historical or cultural interest. These generally begin with visits within the local area. Occasionally, the overzealous parent will drag the very young only child along and wonder in disappointment why the child is disinterested, fretful, or falls asleep. They have not correctly evaluated their child's level of understanding and expect far more interest and attention than a very young child can deliver. Visits to specific sites should be preceded by dicussions about what is about to be seen, its significance and importance. If the parent perceives a lack of enthusiasm or interest in the young child, the trip should be postponed, or the visit will turn into a frustrating day of childhood anger and restlessness and parental frustration and disappointment.

The only child will often think of himself as a piece of extra baggage on trips which ostensibly have been taken to provide him with an educational experience. Such trips may be fun and rewarding for all three people in the family, if honestly planned for the child's enjoyment or enlightenment. A visit to Disneyland may prove as much fun for the parent as for the child. But in reality, that is basically a child-oriented trip and should be balanced by another trip for the parents when the only child is left at home. Often, in the only-child family, every trip is designed so that the child may go along. Fear of separation on the parents' part and a nagging and unrealistic doubt that anyone else can competently care for their child often result in the constant inclusion of the only child on parental vacations. Many parents of only children are aghast that as the child matures, he will refuse to accompany parents on their trips. Often the parents will attribute this behavior to "adolescent rebellion," shake their heads ruefully, and wait for the phase to be lived through. Little do they realize that had they asked the child when he was seven or ten or twelve, they likely would have received the same refusal in a more circumspect, guilty, and confused manner. The child has the right to make decisions and parents have the privilege of independent vacations without their child. It may be painful for the parent of the only child to contemplate but the child may find a vacation from his parents as refreshing and relaxing as the parents do and may be able to work through problems that the parents' immediate presences make difficult for the child to put into the proper perspective.

ENTERTAINMENT

As the child gets older, his scope will broaden and begin to include the movies and, if available, dramatic and musical theater. Again, the parent must be aware that an attention span is necessary to these entertainments. Most films are at least an hour and a half long, and most stage presentations two hours (unless specifically designed for children, when they are half that). Content and manner of presentation should be investigated prior to taking the child so that the parents are neither embarrassed by what is happening on the screen or chagrined at what may be happening by his side in the audience. One of the greatest mistakes that the parent of the only child can make is the assumption that because the child moves somewhat freely and easily in the world of adults, the child is ready for more sophisticated, worldly entertainment of the sort enjoyed and understood by adults. Most small children become confused by the texture of adult entertainment and some feel that they have let their parents down because of their inability to comprehend the story or the meaning or the humor.

The establishment of mutually exclusive life-styles of parent and child, with overlapping when appropriate and convenient, is essential for the child and the parent. Thus, the parent who always includes the only child on all cultural activities is blurring the necessary distinction between two different worlds—the child's and the parents'.

10

Athletics and
the Only Child

A CHILD NEEDS TO EXPLORE athletic activities. He needs to
test himself in each sport, selecting those he enjoys and for
which he has an aptitude. He must be able to experiment in
order to discover his physical strengths and weaknesses and
to learn to use these strengths to their fullest and to overcome
or circumvent the weaknesses. He must have the opportunity
to play with other youngsters and to imitate their behavior,
incorporating what works for him and discarding what does
not.

The natural peer group to introduce the young child to the
world of physical play is his siblings. But obviously the only
child does not have these models to guide him and teach him.
It is therefore up to the only child's parents to perform this
important function. If physical games are used within the
home while the child is very young as a positive, loving form
of expression, the child will not find it difficult to accept the
physical game as a healthy form of interaction. In addition,
sporting events and other demonstrations of physical grace
and prowess should be a part of the extracurricular activities
to which the youngster is exposed. The parents and their
growing child should spend part of their time together in
physical activities such as walking, hiking, ice-skating, roller-
skating, tennis, swimming, even a simple game of catch.
These activities can provide warm, pleasurable communication for both parents and child. They will also stress a noncompetitive, relaxed approach to athletics, rather than a competitive, anxiety-provoking one. The need to excel should be
played down, and the simple joy of physical expression
should be emphasized.

When the child demonstrates an interest in a particular

sport, parents should encourage this interest. Ultimately, the child himself must decide how important a part of his life physical or athletic activities will be. But this decision should be based upon knowledge; the young person should have been given every opportunity to experiment and experience the physical aspects of daily living. After all, we are not all athletes, but we are all physical beings.

AVOIDING STEREOTYPES

Our society still clings to the idea that different levels of athletic activity and accomplishment are appropriate for men and women. The young man is expected to demonstrate a certain degree of assured physical prowess. If he does not, his masculinity is suspect. This is sheer nonsense. Physical or athletic ability is no measure of masculinity. An attempt to live according to such assumptions can lead to considerable unhappiness. A young man may try desperately to conform to this image and may suffer a serious blow to his self-esteem if he is unsuccessful. Or he may engage in athletic activity in order to gain the approval of his peers, although in reality such activity is alien to him. Conversely, another youngster may never move beyond the stereotype of the athletic male, leaving undeveloped the other significant character traits of mature manhood.

A completely opposite image of the young girl has long been dominant. According to this romanticized view, little girls are soft, doll-like creatures. But a young girl must be allowed to explore fully the physical aspects of living; she must have a chance to get dirty, scrape her knee, throw a baseball, climb a tree, and compete with her male peers. The unrealistic concept of delicate womanhood completely overlooks the intense physical demands of bearing and rearing a child, of managing a home or career. Today, men and women are competing in almost every area of life. The young girl who is allowed to participate in sports activities will learn valuable lessons in winning and losing; she will learn to be resilient and to defend herself.

Narrow definitions of masculinity and femininity have no place in today's world. They are relics of a constricted, intolerant past and are best discarded. We are all composed of so-called masculine and feminine traits, but the proportions differ for each individual. Wise parents will not attempt to force discredited and crippling roles on their growing child.

LEARNING THE MEANING OF TEAMWORK

The child who has brothers and sisters has learned to expect the unexpected. He is adept at veering, adjusting, reorienting, and continuing. The only child lacks this experience. He walks onto the playing field literally unschooled in the interactions of individuals striving for a common goal: to win. The only child is unaware that team members may have had to devise individual and group maneuvers to reach that goal. Often, he has not been faced with infighting and the dynamics of team behavior. Consequently, the very young only child may take quite personally the changes of game tactics and the apparent selfish disregard for the individual, all of which is legitimate game-playing behavior and is recognized as such by the other youngsters. The young only child may come home in tears, accusing his playmates of abusing and rejecting him, of considering the game more important than his feelings or safety. Parents must be alert to what is really happening; they should respond by encouraging the child to reenter the game. They should help him to understand the nature of teamwork and the role of the individual as a member of the team. Otherwise, the child may retreat from physical games and move toward less threatening, solitary activities. Such a child will fail to learn important lessons about getting along with others in situations in which he is not the center of attention.

The older only child may react, not by retreating from the action, but by attempting to outmaneuver and outwit the other players. His behavior may become compulsive, even vengeful. This child will plan strategies to get even, or disrupt team function. This will anger the other players, who will recognize it for what it is, regardless of how the only child rationalizes his behavior. They will label him a poor sport, unable to endure normal individual setbacks for the sake of the team's success. To other children, the game is primarily fun; to the overly sensitive only child, the game is a major challenge, almost as important as life itself. He must prove himself; he must outwit and outplay the others; he must be the best.

However, no one can always win, always be the best. That

is why it is essential for the only child to learn to win and lose with dignity. No one enjoys losing, but the only child frequently responds poorly when faced with defeat. He is not accustomed to losing, nor is he prepared for the possibility that he might lose. He lacks experience in giving and compromising. He may overreact, viewing a single loss as a personal condemnation. He must be helped to understand that what is truly important is not the game itself but learning to be gracious in victory and resilient in defeat. The lesson is crucial in the making of a mature adult.

INDIVIDUAL vs. TEAM SPORTS

The only child who is interested in athletics will choose the activity that he finds both physically stimulating and emotionally gratifying and that offers him the greatest opportunity for success and recognition. Because the only child will generally strive to excel and thereby win adult approval, he will often find participation in team sports difficult to adjust to. Team play demands an ability to subordinate individual personality and style to the group effort. Consequently, the only child may move away from team activities.

Sports that emphasize individual accomplishment, such as swimming and track, tend to be more attractive to the athletic only child. He is able to practice and perform on his own and to receive individual attention. He is able to retain his identity; there is no chance that he will be lost in the anonymity of the team. The rewards and recognitions for achievement are his alone. Many only children prefer a sport that combines individual performance with competition, such as tennis or skiing. Tennis, in particular, offers both recognition for individual excellence and the chance to express aggressive impulses in competition.

PARENTAL AMBITIONS AND THE
STAR PHENOMENON

A parent may try to impose unfulfilled dreams of athletic success on the only child. Having failed as an athlete, he or she may see in the child a kind of second chance and hope to bask in the reflected glory of the child's achievements. In some cases, the parent may push the child into a particular sport; in others, the parent may simply make it clear to the child that he is expected to be an outstanding athlete. If the child is unable to fulfill these high expectations (because of lack of motivation, insufficient coordination, or lack of physical ability), both parent and child will view this as a breach of faith, a failure. The child's image of himself may be badly damaged.

Other factors may contribute to an only child's drive for athletic stardom. Because the only child tends to set extremely high standards for himself, nothing short of excellence will be acceptable to him. And the insecure only child may try to use his athletic accomplishments to prove his worthiness to his peer group. He may seek to purchase friendship and acceptance with what he can do, rather than win it for what he is.

Whatever the motivations, the situation is full of danger for the youngster. Athletic stardom is a fleeting thing. If the child has not developed as an individual, he will find himself painfully alone when the cheering has stopped. Once again, sensitive preventive parenting is the key to avoiding such a disaster. Parents must temper the child's drive for success and help him to retain a sense of proportion and to understand that his friendships, family relationships, and self-image must be founded in sturdier, more enduring qualities.

Larry's mother had tried her best to be an ice-skating star. That is what *her* mother wanted. She had taken lessons, entered contests, and tried valiantly, but she never achieved recognition. While Larry was quite young, she attempted to interest him in skating, but he quickly indicated his dislike for the sport. Upset and depressed, his mother discarded her plans for her only son to become the ice-skating star she had not been. However, Larry's mother eventually found the sport for which the boy demonstrated talent. He played tennis unusually well for a ten-year-old.

Lessons involved intense concentration on technique. Mother and son waited almost breathlessly for the professional's assessment at the end of each lesson. Larry soon learned the way to win the approval he needed from his mother was to excel on the tennis court. And so he practiced long and hard to improve his game. After several years of concentrated effort, Larry was playing extremely well. His family moved to a bigger house that had a tennis court so that Larry could practice whenever he had free time. He selected his friends for their ability to play tennis. Schoolwork took second place. Not even weather stopped mother and son; they joined an indoor tennis club. They were a team, sitting on the sidelines, commenting on other players' games, waiting nervously for Larry's turn with the pro.

Soon Larry's mother decided that the local pro was no longer good enough. She located another teacher sixty miles away, and twice weekly the two made the trip so that Larry could have the special lessons. His increasing absorption in the game caused Larry to move away from the few friends that he had developed. By the age of fifteen, he was a loner. His game progressed to the point at which he was considered eligible for a local tournament. In preparation for the matches, he isolated himself from his father and devoted himself to lessons, practice, and critical analysis by his mother. Two weeks before the match, Larry's father left his mother; but as Larry told me later he was so preoccupied with the upcoming matches that he did not react. There was no room for emotion in his rigorous schedule. Only the tournament had any reality for him. His mother missed only a few lessons as she tried to deal with her husband's departure and her only son's preparations.

The day of the competition, fifteen-year-old Larry walked onto the courts to face a much stronger twenty-year-old, who beat him handily in four sets. In defeat, Larry realized that he was truly alone. His friends were gone, his father was gone; his mother was deeply disappointed in him. There was no one with whom to share this loss except his mother, and at that moment, he wanted desperately to avoid her. He quietly walked off the courts, changed his clothes, counted the money in his wallet, slipped out the side door, took a cab to the railroad station, and boarded a train for another city, where he wandered almost penniless for two days before calling home.

Larry's parents sought the help of a marriage counselor and eventually were reunited. But Larry will never be the same young man who walked onto that tennis court that day. He plays tennis infrequently now, and next year, he will go away to a college a good distance from home and from which I suspect he will seldom return. The effort to make him a star was a disaster for Larry and for his parents. His story, although extreme, emphasizes the dangers of imposing the dreams and ambitions of parents on a child.

11

Camp and
the Only Child

GOING AWAY TO CAMP *can* be a frightening and demoralizing experience for an only child. However, if the child has been properly prepared for it by his parents, summer camp can be a vitally important step toward full self-realization. Of course, not every child wants to go to camp, and parents should not attempt to force camp on their youngster if he shows no enthusiasm for the idea. But if a child exhibits deep reluctance to going away to camp, his parents should examine the reasons with great care and sensitivity. The idea of separation may be alarming. And he may lack the self-confidence he needs for successful participation in group activities. Parents should focus on the causes of their child's anxiety and move intelligently to reassure the youngster. The child will then be better prepared not only for a satisfying and beneficial camping experience but also for coping with the challenges of his daily life.

Parents should select a camp that offers a wide range of facilities and activities, so that the child will be able to sample a variety of sports and arts and crafts. There should be a balance of group and individual activities; this will allow the child to explore his leadership potential and to learn to use his spare time sensibly and pleasurably. In addition, parents should take the time to meet the staff and examine their qualifications. After all, these people will be responsible for the care of the child for an extended period of time. I have always been distressed when parents ship their child off to camp without ever having met the director, discussed the camp facilities, or visited the campsite.

Many extremely valuable experiences await the only child during a stay at summer camp. The group activities may give the youngster added self-confidence, and this may reveal or enhance his leadership qualities. The friendships he forms may be deep and gratifying. For the only child, this may be the summer's greatest pleasure. Knowing that he has the ability to make friends can give the only child inner strength, confidence, and a sense of himself as a worthwhile and wanted human being.

Most importantly, summer camp allows the only child to test himself in a relaxed atmosphere, away from the judgmental eyes of his parents. The greatest benefit an only child can get from a camping experience is the realization that he can succeed on his own. One summer of independence, of self-reliance, can go a very long way toward showing the only child that he is capable of shaping his own future. He will learn that he can accept whatever he may need from his parents without being totally dependent on them.

PROBLEM OF SEPARATION

When parents decide to send their only child to summer camp, they must realize that separation may present problems for the youngster. The child will be better prepared to cope with separation if he has spent some time away from his parents before his first trip to summer camp. Therefore, parents should arrange for the child to visit relatives who live some distance away. Even brief visits with relatives or friends in the same city will help the child in adjusting to a more extended separation from parents and home. In addition, parents should encourage their only child to spend the night at a friend's or relative's home whenever possible. All these experiences will provide the youngster with a reassuring preview of the camping experience and will help him to adjust to that more dramatic separation.

If the parents of an only child recognize that their relationship with their youngster has been too intense and that they have done too much as a threesome, they must gently begin to spend time away from the child. A good way to start is by going out more frequently in the evening without the child. Also, they should take occasional short vacation trips by themselves. The only child must recognize that his parents have a life of their own, a life apart from the one they share with him. He must learn to accept periods of separation as normal and nonthreatening.

Once the child is at camp, I urge parents to take advantage of visiting day. But they must be especially careful to maintain the proper attitude during these visits. The worst thing for the child is a tearful greeting from dependent parents obviously upset by the long separation. No matter how much they miss their child, they must respect his right and need to become independent. Such behavior will show the only child how much he is missed. And if the child has begun to adapt and does not miss his parents to an equally dramatic degree, he may develop a sense of guilt and a belief that it is wrong to be away from his parents.

PROBLEM OF HOMESICKNESS

One problem faced by the only child when he first goes to camp is shared by many first-time campers: homesickness. This is a very natural reaction to their first time far away from home for an extended period. But for the only child the separation is likely to be more acutely felt and more painful. As the children who have brothers or sisters begin to settle into the camp experience, they will recognize certain patterns of peer relationships that are not too different from those within their own families. Counselors are rather like older siblings; the younger children in camp are rather like younger siblings. The give-and-take of these relationships is much like that which they have experienced at home. For these youngsters, camp takes on a reassuring familiarity and yet remains sufficiently different from home to be exciting.

For the only child, however, camp is a strange world. Consequently, adaptation is usually slow. The only child may take days or weeks to warm up to and accept the various aspects of the camp experience. Parents, counselors, and camp directors must recognize this pattern for what it is and remain patient. Parents may receive frantic phone calls or letters filled with desperate pleas for rescue. Their response should be sympathetic, but they must always express their confidence in the child's ability to make a happy adjustment to camp. Any impetuous action to remove the child from the camp in response to these cries of distress is unwise and potentially damaging to the child's future development. An abortive camp experience may have unhealthy influence on the only child's later decisions concerning group activities, vacations away from his family, and the selection of a college and career.

PROBLEM OF INDIVIDUALITY

During his first days at camp, a child experiences an almost complete loss of his individual identity. He becomes a member of various groups that are identified according to bunk, according to age and size. Teams are selected at random. Meals are communal events. This process can be quite frightening to an only child. He is likely to be confused and angry, and he is generally unprepared for this experience.

But gradually, the process reverses itself. The child gains recognition for individual characteristics, actions, achievements, and special talents. He becomes identifiable by his function as a team member and by his new friendships. By the time he is ready to go home, each child has been tested, measured, categorized, and usually accepted as an individual. He has developed a definite identity. When parents come to take their child home, they often find that he has acquired a strange nickname, that he is extolled for virtues and teased about weaknesses they know nothing about. He may hardly seem the same child who left for camp a few short weeks before. Parents and counselors should advise the only child to work patiently to develop his best qualities so that the identity he achieves at camp will be accepted and respected by his peers. The only child who pouts, who reacts immaturely, who refuses to adapt, who balks at friendship, who shuns new experiences will indeed have an identity by the time he leaves camp, but it will bring him only scorn and rejection from his peers. This can seriously damage the way the child feels about himself.

The camping experience is extremely important for what it will indicate about the way in which the maturing only child will adapt to the world outside his home. If he is unable to get along with other youngsters within the camp environment, he may repeat the same negative patterns in later life.

Adaptation can, of course, be taught. But parents must not rely on summer camp to do the job for them. They must begin to teach their only child to adapt to other children, to adjust to the outside world, to develop an acceptable and independent identity long before the day the youngster first leaves for camp. If they fail to meet this responsibility, their child's future may be irreparably damaged.

If a youngster's first camp experience is an unhappy one, parents should not try to explain it away by blaming the other youngsters, the camp staff, or anyone or anything else. Such a reaction may be momentarily reassuring, but it cannot help the child. Parents in this situation should examine their child's maladaptive behavior as carefully and objectively as possible and do whatever is necessary to correct any mistakes in the way they have been raising the child.

WHAT PARENTS CAN EXPECT AND LEARN FROM CAMP

Parents sometimes expect that the camp experience will change their child dramatically in a brief period of time. The quiet child is expected to be gregarious; the clumsy child, to excel in athletics; the passive child, to be more forceful; the irresponsible, pampered child, to demonstrate responsibility and self-reliance. Four weeks of summer camp cannot be expected to work miraculous changes or undo the damage inflicted by misguided parents. What camp *can* do is give the youngster the beginnings of self-confidence and self-reliance. Parents must encourage their child to build upon this foundation when he comes home from camp. If the child has demonstrated positive changes in personality and behavior at camp, parents should make every effort to learn what it is in the camp environment that has brought about this growth. They can learn a great deal about their child's feelings and needs, strengths and weaknesses from the adults who have been responsible for the youngster during his stay at camp. They should be receptive and willing to adjust their child-rearing methods in ways that will help their child to become a mature, independent adult. Camp can be an invaluable educational experience for the only child *and* for his parents.

A DIVIDEND FOR PARENTS

Parents of an only child may become so absorbed in their child and in their roles as parents that they neglect their growth as individuals and as marriage partners. When they send the child to camp, they give themselves an excellent opportunity to look at themselves and their marriage. They will have time to discuss, to resolve, to strengthen. A vacation from parenting can be a time for adjustment and growth.

12

Beauty and
the Only Child

BECAUSE THE ONLY CHILD HAS the whole of the parental
ambitions, expectations and future fantasies invested completely in him, physical appearance can very easily become
an obsession and lead to continuous, debilitating self-depreca-
tion and lack of self-esteem on the part of the plain or perhaps even unattractive youngster. One is not surprised when
the physical beauty of the female child is stressed, but males
are not exempt from such attention. The male only child is
watched carefully to make certain that his features are attractive, that he does not scar his face during play, that he
does not suffer the usual adolescent acne, that his body is
neither too thin nor too heavy, and that he grows tall enough.
Often the concern is extreme.

Mrs. M. brought her eighteen-month-old son in for his
checkup and, during the examination, made a point to ask
me to check his ears. I examined them carefully, found the
ear canals and drums quite healthy and told her so. She
sniffed angrily and asked me to assess the outer ears. The
boy had moderately prominent ears which stood out from
his head and appeared slightly conspicuous because of his
thin, late developing hair. I took my time with this only son,
then turned and attempted to reassure the mother that the
external ears, though moderately large, were well formed
and would not be a physical detriment once the facial bones
expanded fully during maturation and the child's hair grew
to its fullest length. She stared at me and finally asked in a
clear and very direct voice, "When can they be fixed?"

I paused, then said, "I would certainly wait. So much more
growing and changing has to occur. And surgery has its psychic effects on every youngster."

She nodded and smiled. I felt I had made my point and finished the examination, wrote out the instructions and chatted easily. As she dressed the young child, she turned toward me.

"Would you be kind enough to write down the name of a qualified plastic surgeon? His father and I do not wish to wait."

I gave her the name of an excellent surgeon whom I suspected would have the same attitude about the premature and unnecessary surgery that I did. And I was right. This did not dampen the determination of these parents to make their only son "perfect." They shopped around from surgeon to surgeon until at twenty-three months, the child underwent surgery to fix his slightly protuberant ears. The terrible irony was that the boy grew to develop a broad, high cheek boned, very handsome, masculine face with only one significant flaw—tiny, feminine ears that appeared incongruous with the full, heavily boned features of his maturing face.

Cosmetic dental work and many physically painful procedures are not uncommon. The only child who is not physically attractive to the degree expected by the parents is usually actuely aware of the physical failings in the parents' eyes. The subject may be openly discussed or tacitly alluded to. But, no matter how the information is transmitted, it is quite rare for the only child not to be very sensitive to parental reactions and, by extension, the outside world.

There are several areas where the only child must cope with parental overambition and overinvestment: athletics, education, and creativity. But what can unattractive only children do to overcome the features with which they were born? There is no practice, no lesson, no study that will improve his basic features. The child is simply helpless in the face of overt or covert parental disapproval of his physical appearance.

There is an obvious and clear-cut solution to this dilemma. The parents of the only child must accept their offspring as an individual whom they care for and nuture and guide toward maturity. Outward physical beauty is a thin façade covering the complex inner self. It has little more significance than the beautiful face of a watch.

It is imperative for the parents of the only child not to set up standards of personal appearance or beauty which their child cannot possibly hope to attain. The child will suffer from a sense of personal ugliness, will feel that his lack of beauty has more importance than his inner qualities, and will develop attitudes that place an inappropriate emphasis on physical appearance.

One related problem is the subtle and unrecognized danger of developing an overconcentration on the trappings that replace or enhance the physical appearance of the child—clothing. Too often the only child becomes a "clothes horse," constantly dragged from one children's store to the next, rarely being allowed the privilege of getting dirty or looking disheveled in old, favorite clothes. The attractive child receives clothing as a reward for beauty, and the plain only child will be dressed in the most expensive clothes the family budget can afford in order to cover, minimize, distract from, and possibly even soften the impact of the child's plainness. This clothing syndrome becomes distorted and the child is treated as if he or she were a baby doll. All parents should take note: outward beauty deserves far less of the parents' time than the nuturing of inner qualities.

13
Health, the Doctor, and the Only Child

No MATTER How CAREFULLY parents may plan, no matter how diligently they may care for their children, some episodes of ill health are inevitable. Nevertheless, there is a normal tendency for parents to experience some feelings of guilt when their youngster becomes ill. "What did I do wrong that might have caused this?" and "How could I have prevented this?" are common questions. The sickness need not be serious or life threatening to elicit this type of response from parents; the simplest cold or low-grade fever may prompt them to reassess their child-care methods. Regardless of the fact that they have little direct control over the occurrence of childhood illnesses, most parents will blame themselves. This is particularly true of parents who lack child-rearing experience; that is, parents of a first or only child.

These parents will search for errors or oversights that may have caused the illness. Even the most minor or unrelated incidents may seem significant. The result is that the child's range of permitted activities decreases; at the same time, parents may impose increasingly rigid rules and regulations regarding such matters as eating habits, sleeping hours, clothing, group play, and crowds. Most only children are likely to have to contend with minor, often irrational limitations, depending on the nature of the most recent illness, but a small number of only children suffer from pathological restriction of their activities. It is important for parents of only children to remember that they are not diagnosticians. Limits imposed on a child's life without consultation with a pediatrician or family doctor may do the child far more harm in the long run than a normal, transient childhood illness.

In my experience, parents of an only child are more likely

91

to jump to hasty conclusions and to overestimate the seriousness of their child's condition. For example, many parents of
only children bring their youngsters to me for a tonsillectomy
after a winter of the age-appropriate quota of colds and sore
throats. Such overreaction is to be expected because these
parents will not have sufficient experience to recognize a normal pattern of winter illnesses. Parents who have several children expect some minor toeing-in at two years and some
bowing at four years, but parents of an only child are likely
to seek immediate treatment from an orthopedic specialist.
Usually, the pediatrician can calm the parents by patiently
explaining the normal problems a growing child will experience. But sometimes no amount of reassurance will help, and
the overly anxious parents will drag the youngster to a number of specialists before they realize that time will be the best
healer for such minor abnormalities.

DEALING WITH PARENTAL ANXIETY

Of course, parents cannot help being worried when their
child is ill; after all, the child's health is in jeopardy. This
reaction is perfectly normal. But parents of an only child, because of their inexperience, may be unable to see a given
illness in the proper perspective. Consequently, their concern
may be extreme, even hysterical.

Such a reaction can be very alarming to the child because
a child naturally looks to his parents to provide calm, intelligent care when he is ill. If he sees that his parents are overly
anxious and frightened, he will begin to lose confidence in
their ability to care for him. This, in turn, can make any
illness even more frightening for the child.

How well I remember my own parents hovering nervously
near my bed whenever I was ill. I had my forehead felt so often that until I grew up, I thought the gesture was an ethnic
sign of affection. The thermometer and I became intimate
friends. I was put to bed for the sprains, strains, cuts, and
bruises that are a normal part of the hazards of everyday
play for a growing boy. As I grew older, I learned to hide
these small and insignificant daily injuries from my overly
concerned parents. During my fifth year, I had survived a
very serious case of pneumonia that had required hospitaliza-
tion. Thereafter, my parents viewed each minor cold, each
unimportant pain or injury as the possible precursor of an-

other major health crisis. They had come close to losing their only child, and they relived that experience with each new illness, no matter how insignificant. At first, I shared their deep fears; but gradually, I sensed that their concern was extreme, and began to dismiss their evaluations of my complaints and rely more upon my own judgment. I had to dispense with that comfortable dependency most children retreat into during illness. As an adolescent, I found myself reassuring my parents about the relatively minor illnesses I suffered. Our roles were reversed; I had become the health counselor and educator of my parents because they were unable to cope with their own fears and to place my illnesses in the appropriate perspective.

It is extremely difficult to ease the fears of the only child's parents. They may be plagued with the idea that the child will die. Even a minor illness may seem to them to have the potential for causing serious harm. Nevertheless, regardless of how worried they may be about their child's illness, parents must do everything they can not to let the child see their concern, even if this means a major playacting effort. Even when faced with a serious childhood disease, parents must hide their feelings. The ailing child is already sufficiently frightened by pain, rashes or swellings, fever, and other sensations that are part of his illness. He needs to be able to look to calm, confident parents to soothe his discomfort and to reassure him.

At this point, I would like to add an extra bit of advice. Disease and death are not generally topics of conversation among children. But the only child is surrounded by adults much of the time. It is therefore wise for parents to take care not to become involved in discussion of the illnesses of friends or their own parents when the child is present. If such topics are a major element of the conversations a child hears every day, it can only encourage excessive concern about health matters that could seriously distort the young child's view of the world.

CONSEQUENCES OF PARENTAL ANXIETY

When parents are unable to control or at least conceal their excessive concern about their only child's health, the youngster may develop a complementary maladaptive response.

The child may experience constant fear of illness and recurrent imagined sicknesses (hypochondria). He has learned these responses from his overconcerned parents, whose anxieties have focused his attention on his health. Inevitably, such a child begins to wonder and worry about his physical well-being. After all, if his parents are constantly so concerned, there must be some valid reason for alarm. The child may begin to imagine that every minor illness or injury is major. In a serious case of childhood hypochondriasis, the youngster may develop such vague but suggestive symptoms as abdominal pain, headache, chest pain, and weakness. The solution to the problem does not lie in proving to the child that the illness is indeed imaginary; the illness will only be replaced by another that is equally worrisome. Furthermore, the child will begin to lose faith in his doctor's ability to diagnose his repeated illnesses correctly and to help him. Instead, the child must be helped to realize that his extreme concern with his health is based, not on reality, but on the constant anticipatory fears and concerns of his parents.

Henry, a sixteen-year-old only child, walked into my office one Saturday morning and announced that he was convinced he had stomach cancer. During his childhood, he had watched the prolonged suffering of his terminally ill grandmother. Henry's every injury or sickness was cause for intense maternal anxiety. During the past year, he had been to my office on numerous occasions, each time convinced that he had a fatal illness. Each time, I examined and tested as thoroughly as was appropriate and sensible, and he would calm down. But a month or two later, he would return with a new complaint. Within an hour of each visit, Henry's mother would call to ask if her son had the disease that they both had feared he had. Private consultations with Henry's mother did little to shake her conviction that the health of her deeply loved son was in danger.

On this particular Saturday, I gave Henry a thorough physical examination and again reassured him that his fears were groundless. However, I recommended that he seek psychiatric help to resolve his disabling concern about his health. He took my advice and consulted a psychiatrist. But soon Henry was caught in a desperate struggle between the realities that the psychiatrist was asking him to face and the tightly constructed fantasy world of illness and dependency in which he and his mother lived. He believed that if he accepted the fact that his illnesses were indeed imaginary, he would be rejecting his mother. This was too much for Henry to do and too much for his mother to allow; he stopped therapy. Shortly thereafter, he dropped out of school because of recurrent absences. Today, Henry goes from doctor to doctor, seeking validation of his complaints. He is jobless, unhappy, and constantly suffering from imaginary diseases.

Henry's is an extreme case, a sad and pitiful waste of human life. However, there are many gradations of hypochondriacal behavior. This emotional disorder is both frequent among only children and preventable. Everything depends on the attitudes and behavior of the parents.

Another response to extreme parental concern involves the child's use of illness to get his own way. Because he is acutely aware of the importance his parents place upon his health, the only child may complain of a stomachache, headache, or sore throat in order to avoid school, unpleasant tasks, household responsibilities, or potentially threatening or challenging situations. More significantly, he may use such complaints to monopolize his parents' attention. Of course, these lessons are learned very early by most children. But parents of more than one child are less easily manipulated and more assured in assessing the child's physical complaints. There is a very real danger that the only child will continue to use physical symptoms as a method of avoidance or as a means of gaining attention in later life. As an adult, such an only child may find false symptoms an easy way to hide from the expectations and demands of the outside world.

HOME REMEDIES

Because of their lack of knowledge and previous experience, the parents of an only child may turn to the only other people they know who have had direct experience with childhood illnesses: their own parents. They may not even have to ask for advice. Grandparents often feel that they are experts in all areas of child-rearing, including illness, and they may attempt to take charge of the situation when their grandchild is ill. Parents must not permit such intrusions. I do not mean to condemn a request for assistance from a willing grandparent. Nor do I wish to denigrate the deep concern that grandparents feel for an ailing grandchild. But neither their concern nor their assistance should be allowed to lead to excessive involvement in the care of the child. There are several reasons for this.

First, the parents of an only child will never learn to care for their youngster if they constantly depend on others. It is only through involvement in the day-to-day care of the child, guided by the child's pediatrician, that the parents will acquire the knowledge and skill to feel capable of dealing with subsequent illnesses. Furthermore, if grandparents take charge of the child's care, the role of the parents will be diminished in the child's eyes.

Second, medications and methods of treatment have changed dramatically since the grandparents' child-rearing years. Consequently, the recommendations made by the well-meaning grandparents may be obsolete and even dangerous. I am deeply concerned about the use of outmoded or family cures for childhood illness. The results can be tragic. A young couple had been away for two days; during that time, they had left their infant son in the care of his maternal grandmother. When they returned, they found that the child had developed gastrointestinal symptoms and moderately severe diarrhea. The grandmother had not called me. Instead, she had prepared a thick, salted turkey soup, which she proceeded to substitute for the child's regular feedings. This treatment had been used in her family for generations. The young mother found her child fretful, not eating well, and having frequent loose stools. Although the young woman and her husband (who was a dental student) recognized the potential seriousness of their baby's condition, the grandmother convinced them to continue her treatment over the weekend. They kept reheating the soup, thus evaporating more water. The mixture became thicker; the salt content, more and more concentrated. By Monday morning, the infant was desperately ill. Only then did the frightened young mother call me. The baby was rushed to the hospital, where immediate steps were taken to save him. But the salt level within his serum was lethal, and irreversible damage had occurred. The child died hours later of salt poisoning.

SHARING CHILD-CARE RESPONSIBILITIES

In many cases, both parents of an only child are deeply committed to careers. Therefore, dealing with childhood illnesses may present special problems. Which parent should stay at home when their child is ill? Who should be called if the child becomes ill or is injured at school? Too often, the mother automatically assumes all these responsibilities. But this is nonsense. If men and women are ever going to free themselves from the restrictions of narrowly defined sex roles, this is an excellent and important area in which to begin. When both parents have demanding jobs, the responsibility of caring for their sick only child must be shared. There will be times when pressures at work will make it impossible for one parent to stay at home with the child or take the child to the doctor's office. Then, the other parent should adjust his or her work schedule accordingly. Such sharing may be arranged on a day-to-day basis or perhaps for longer periods of time. No rigid schedules need be set up, but neither parent should have to assume total child-care. Such sharing conveys a very healthy and comfortable message to the child: namely, that both parents are concerned enough and competent enough to care for him during an illness.

ROLE OF THE PHYSICIAN

As their children grow, parents who have more than one child acquire a good deal of knowledge about childhood illnesses and considerable ability to deal with them. They learn to recognize what is to be expected at various ages, what is minor and can be managed without the doctor's attention, and what is unusual and potentially dangerous. They come to know what methods of treatment of the usual childhood diseases have worked for their other children. But parents of an only child must face each new illness and each new growth period, with its special physical and emotional problems, with little or no experience to draw upon. The pediatrician can expect far more phone calls and office visits from the parents of an only child than he would from parents who have several children. This is altogether understandable.

Therefore, the pediatrician is extremely important to the only-child family. He or she has to be more than a healer; he or she must be the parents' health educator and counselor. The physician can be of immeasurable help to the parents of an only child by recommending appropriate books and by discussing usual childhood diseases *before* they occur. When the child is ill, the physician should spend as much time as is necessary to explain to them the meaning and the importance of each sign and symptom. They will be better able to judge the seriousness of a future illness if they know, for example, which fevers, rashes, and deviations in usual respiratory, urinary, or bowel patterns are significant and which are not.

Unfortunately, not all physicians understand the importance of developing parental self-confidence. They may create a dependent relationship that cripples the parents' ability to care for their child's health needs. When my oldest daughter was quite young, she had severe colic. Because I was on duty as a pediatric intern for a good part of that chaotic time, my wife had to deal with the problem on her own. After some sleepless nights and fretful days for both mother and child, she called the pediatrician. He gave her strict instructions and told her to call back the next day. Each day the instructions changed; each day she had to call him almost from feeding to feeding to report and to receive new advice. Her efforts to adapt to the constantly changing instructions created considerable tension, and the baby's colic increased dramatically. What my wife needed from the physician was a calming, intelligent discussion about what to expect and how to deal with it. A new pediatrician and a new approach soon solved the problem.

Parents who have more than one child are familiar with the minor emotional disruptions that normally occur as a child grows and struggles to achieve maturity. They have lived through the two-year-old's negative rebellion, the four-year-old's assertions of individuality, the six-year-old's experiments with lying and stealing. But to parents of a first or only child, these appear to be very serious emotional disturbances. They may conclude that the problem is their fault. In this area, too, the physician can help parents to understand the many variations of experimental behavior that a child must go through on his journey to emotional maturity.

Finally, parents and physician must make every effort to help the only child become self-sufficient in dealing with minor injuries and illnesses. The more the youngster feels in control of his own body, the more confident he will be of his ability to handle crises and make rational decisions about his own health and the less likely he will be to face illness or injury with fear and excessive concern.

14

Sex Education and the Only Child

THE ONLY CHILD FACES TWO DISTINCT disadvantages in the area of sex education: the absence of siblings and the difficulty with peer-group relationships. Each of these eliminates essential areas of exposure and contact that often prove helpful in initiating thought and investigation into sexual knowledge at the appropriate time.

First, the only child has not had the opportunity to be faced with the biologic fact and considerations of maternal pregnancy within the family unit. Secondly, the only child has no siblings to question, to use as body models, and to share stories with.

As to the first of these disadvantages, the parent of the only child need not allow opportunity to be lost. There are often a number of pregnant friends within the mother's social circle. Exposure to several of these pregnant women will usually initiate the type of questions that permit open discussion of the process of fetal growth, the sexual overtones, and the birth procedure. If, after repeated exposure to pregnancy no inquiries are forthcoming, then it may well be because the child fails to perceive that pregnancy is relevant to his daily life, since it has not been part of his own family unit. Small children can be strongly concrete beings. So the absence of questions is rarely because of the child avoiding the subject, but merely due to his failure to associate the relevance of the subject with himself. Here the mother should point out the condition of pregnancy to the only child and open the topic for brief but meaningful discussion to be followed by repeated exposures with, hopefully, a heightened interest and more spontaneous questioning.

Siblings share the delicious secrets of intimate sexual behavior as they learn and transmit the choice bits of exciting information from peers or the media. Though often exaggerated or distorted, the transmission of the sexual information piques the interest of the child and moves him to seek out more information either from peer, sibling, or parent. The only child does not have this added motivational and educational force. There are no siblings to view or to share information with or to go to for more about street stories.

Only children are usually not group children; they function far better in tight singular or small group clusters. These singular friendships are often with children very much like themselves, not infrequently other only children. Therefore, the two friends share the same level of ignorance about the area of sex information and low level of curiosity about matters pertaining to sexual behavior. By often excluding the remainder of the peer group in favor of tight singular bonding, the only children eliminate the group interchange relative to sexual subjects, no matter how distorted; and the only children remain understimulated and badly informed.

The irony of the problem relative to early sexual knowledge is that the child moves so frequently in the adult society where subjects pertaining to sexual situations are often openly discussed in his presence because his level of knowledge and sophistication is assumed to be at a higher level than it actually is. The only child, therefore, often develops a vocabulary without definitions, phrases without meaning, concepts he parrots without the basic facts understood and assimilated. Thus the only child might sound quite worldly compared to his peer group when engaged in conversations about sex, but the actual knowledge is no deeper than a sketchy familiarity with the language of sexual matters rather than a full and healthy understanding. The adult society, which often finds the only child lingering within its midst, should be aware that the child is not sufficiently mature to understand and make judgments on sexual matters overheard in adult company. Therefore, the parents should attempt to minimize his contact and exposure to cocktail party chatter and dinner party conversations. Also, the parent can tactfully change the subject when sexual topics and references begin to flow all around and over the head of the hapless, naïve child. He may not be ready to assimilate the meaning of the language that he hears. If so, then he should not be exposed to it. If the only child is so exposed, the parents must be prepared to discuss and clarify misconceptions and questions as quickly as possible.

Obviously, for the only child, the key figures in early and subsequent sexual education will be the parents. This places certain distinct responsibilities upon the parent. The first is very clear—to be well informed. This is good, solid advice for all parents, since parents are generally extremely important as "front-line" sex educators even in multiple-child families. The parents should investigate and learn the sex information necessary to be the best teachers in intimate human behavior that they can be. This may require taking books from the library at the librarian's suggestion; contacting Planned Parenthood organizations for pamphlets, books, and visuals; asking the pediatrician or gynecologist for the name of appropriate texts; or discussing with them subjects about which the parents themselves are confused or concerned. Courses are being offered at many of the local colleges in sexual education which may fit the bill for one or both parents, to inform them of subjects about which they know little and refresh their information on others about which they feel reasonably comfortable. The world *comfortable* is a terribly important one when we deal with the sexual education of the young. The parent must give evidence to the young person during the times that they are advising and educating that they themselves are at ease with the subject—informed and not embarrassed. The overall impression upon the young person will be positive rather than negative. If the parent is visibly concerned or ill-informed, then the youngster's response will either be concerned or withdrawn. This comfort in discussing sexual behavior comes from an informed base. The more we know, the less threatening the subject. So the first step for the parent of the only child (for any parent, for that matter) is to become as informed and up-to-date on the modern thoughts and philosophies about intimate human behavior as possible.

The second responsibility for the parents of the only child is to avoid developing a relationship so intensely intimate with the youngster that they become embarrassed to discuss sexual matters with their own child. The intense parent-child relationships which occasionally develop in only-child households can reach levels which are essentially unhealthy and confuse the child with the unresolved Oedipal overtones. When a relationship between a parent and only child has reached a point where the discussions of sexual issues cause intense embarrassment to parent and child, then a careful and honest reassessment of the interaction must be made to avoid the subsequent obvious problems of separation, marriage, and dependency.

Thirdly, the parent of the only child must be acutely aware of the fact that when the child reaches the adolescent period and dramatic body changes and sudden emergence of libido drives occur, that the only child may have only the parent to turn to for advice. Children from multiple families may have watched the changes in siblings, discussed or observed the changing drives, or shared with peers their own adolescent conversions. They find comfort in similarities and normal differences. But the only child usually will not share this information as readily with a group or even a peer friend. The parent must be on the alert to detect the emergence of puberty and the normal concurrent changes. Much discussion relative to the expectations of body and psychic change should have antedated the actual pubertal changes. However, when they begin, attempts to reintroduce the subject to allow for questioning and honest and reassuring answers should be undertaken. The parent of the late developing only child should also be sensitive to the problems. These youngsters are often smaller than their peer group during this period of their life which is an added detraction from overt acceptance and involvement. They also feel "different." The other girls are wearing bras; the other boys have deeper voices. Gym showers are dreaded; physical education avoided. These are the signals. These youngsters need the reassurance from the parent that adolescent development is not a homogenous affair, an all-or-none explosion, but occurs at a different pace and time in each child with the ultimate result being the same within certain normal height-weight variations. If the late developing child feels deep concern about his or her lack of maturation and seriously questions the "pat" answers given by the reassuring parent, then a visit to the pediatrician or to the gynecologist will likely solve the immediate concerns of the child because of the professional weight of the medical opinion.

When dealing with an only child, how should the parent approach the subject of sexual education? By allowing the child to discover his or her self. The parent should permit the normal child investigation of his own body—every orifice and appendage. One of the most inhibiting problems is the parent who slaps the infant's hand while he is exploring his genitalia or anal area. This signifies that these areas are not to be explored. They are "off limits." Ultimately, they will be viewed as "dirty." The freedom to explore one's own body is the very beginning of healthy sexual education.

Next, the parents of the only child should be somewhat flexible in the limits of the privacy within their own home. This is not to suggest that nudity and provocative disrobing is the approach to the sexual education of the child. But the natural openness of bedroom doors when parents are dressing or disrobing will give the child free access to satisfy the momentary curiosity without suggesting invitation. Again the closing of doors or the reprimanding of the child who suddenly appears as the parent is dressing only emphasizes the "secrecy" and possibly the "shame" of the human body.

As a parent, it is essentially an honor to be the first other person your child experiences and accepts. There is nothing sexual in a child viewing a parent disrobed or naked; it is merely the satisfaction of human curiosity. The concern about appearing naked in front of a young child, unfortunately, lies within the embarrassed and confused mind of the parent. The only-child parents can, by being natural and comfortable about themselves, give to their child the first sense of the other person which is natural and nonthreatening. Answering the child's questions becomes part of that experience. Such questions as "Why do you have hair there and I don't?" or "What is that thing?" are questions requiring honest but basic answers at the level of the child's understanding. Open, natural discussions concerning sexual subjects by the family will give the only child an inner sense of comfort and ease in bringing the subject up with the parents when points of confusion arise as they so often do during the maturational period. There should be no question which does not dignify a response nor any discussion which cannot be phrased in language and context that is relevant to the age and understanding of the particular child.

As the only child grows into young adulthood, the parents should bring recommended texts into the home for the young person to read, if desired. As the only child matures into adolescence, the decision-making as to what sexual information will be shared with the parent, what sexual questions will be asked of the parent, and what sexual problems will be brought to the parent becomes the personal decision of the young developing adult himself. At this age, the teen years, the foundation should be there for the child's acceptance of sex as a natural biologic entity which carries the burden of responsibility for oneself and the other person. The atmosphere should permit direct, specific answers relative to the acts of intimate human behavior. If this has been accomplished by the parent of the only child, then the questions asked and the problems presented will be shared intimacies and consultations—with parents whose approach to the problems of sexuality has indicated a willingness to be honest, free, open, and unashamed.

15

The Adolescent
Only Child

THE DIFFICULT PERIOD OF ADOLESCENCE marks the precarious journey from childhood to maturity. It is fraught with problems and delays. Unless his parents handle this phase intelligently and sensitively, the young person may never complete the trip.

Because adolescence is the time of greatest rebellion, it is also the time of the highest risk of serious and even permanent damage to the parent-child relationship. The teen-ager will question or discard the ideas and the philosophy of his parents in order to examine and test them for himself. He will reject the family life-style and traditions. For example, he may refuse to attend a birthday, anniversary, or other special celebration that has always been an important event for the family as a unit. Such a decision gives the young person a chance to weigh his own feelings, both feelings about being absent from an important family function and feelings of independence arising from this break with tradition. It is vital that the young person experience forms of behavior that differ from his own past patterns as well as from those of his family and his peer group. In this way, he will be able to evaluate alternatives and choose what suits him best as an individual. This is an extremely important step in the formation of a clear concept of self.

This necessary rejection of family ideas and life-style is often extremely difficult for parents to accept. Those who have several children soon learn to accept their teen-agers' behavior for what it is and to wait patiently for it to pass. But parents of an only (or first) child, because of their lack of experience, are likely to be alarmed by the adolescent's normal drawing away, which they regard as threatening their close relationship with their child. They view the teenager's rejection of family styles and values as a rejection of *them* and may conclude that they have failed as parents.

These parents may attempt to rekindle the young person's enthusiasm for family activities, and they may demand adherence to family routines. But such painful and unnecessary confrontations can only result in intensified rebellion and rejection. In other cases, the parents may come to the conclusion that they have lost their child. The resulting feelings of guilt and the inevitable recriminations can seriously damage their marriage and therefore the source of the child's emotional support, the family unit itself. When the adolescent's rebellion has run its course, the young person will have no family foundation to return to.

Clearly, it is extremely important for parents to be prepared for their adolescent's move away from the family. They must not feel that they have been rejected when the young person turns to his peers for advice. Parents must fully understand their role in this painful period of dramatic transformation. They must learn to roll with the punches, to be tolerant, to watch and wait. If they can recall their own tribulations during adolescence, it may help them to put their child's behavior in proper perspective. They must remain available to give advice and solace, but they must never interfere. This is difficult, especially for parents of an only child, but it is essential both for the child's emotional growth and for the health of the parent-child relationship.

A SURROGATE FAMILY

The child who has older brothers or sisters has had the opportunity to observe how they have reacted to the troubles and the challenges of adolescence. The same may be said of a child who has grown up in an extended-family environment in which he has been able to observe cousins, aunts, and uncles during their teen-age years. But the only child rarely has the benefit of such behavior models. For him, everything about this complex period is new, and every action or adjustment is experimental. Consequently, it is not unusual for the only child to look elsewhere for the examples that his home environment cannot provide.

When she brought Susan, her sixteen-year-old only child, to my office for a checkup, Mrs. H. asked if she might speak with me privately. "What is troubling you?" I asked. Mrs. H. blurted out, "She keeps talking about wanting to move out and go to live with her girl friend's family. She says that they understand her better than we do." "Is it a large family?" I asked. Mrs. H. smiled and answered, "They have five kids, all ten or older. They wouldn't have any room for her. Why does she want to go and stay in such a madhouse?"

I explained that it is not unusual for an only child to yearn for a large family. During adolescence, this may go beyond the fantasy stage. The adolescent only child may actually select a surrogate family, usually one with a number of older children. Generally, the parents in such a family are accustomed to the variabilities and unpredictabilities of adolescence, but they also adhere to firm basic rules and regulations of appropriate social behavior and to principles of self-discipline and responsibility. To the adolescent only child, this may seem to be an ideal family. He will often spend most of his time at this adopted home, observing and learning the varieties of acceptable individual and social behavior.

The only child's parents must understand that all the young person is doing is searching for examples of different behavior patterns and methods of handling situations so that he can make decisions on the basis of a broader knowledge than his own family experience is able to offer. They should not feel that their own close-knit family has been disrupted or that they are engaged in a competition with the surrogate family for the only child's love and loyalty. Rather, they should encourage this search for alternatives.

Other kinds of groups that can provide the only child with alternative models include scouts, church groups, clubs or fraternal organizations, extracurricular activities (such as debating societies, drama clubs, and team sports), and summer camp. The only child should be encouraged to participate in such group activities. The development of a broader knowledge of the diversity of human behavior will prove invaluable to the only child in making intelligent decisions with regard to his own behavior and life-style.

PRIVACY

During the teen-age years, the question of privacy is often the cause of dissension in the home of the only child. The adolescent only child begins to spend a considerable amount of time by himself, often behind closed doors. Telephone conversations are conducted in the privacy of the teen-ager's room, often in purposefully hushed tones and punctuated with peals of laughter. The young adult may become quite uncommunicative, speaking seldom and volunteering as little information as possible about his daily life and his evening activities. Too many questions from his well-meaning parents are likely to be greeted with intense anger.

This strong desire for privacy is common to all adolescents, but it is likely to cause particularly painful conflict in the home of an only child because the parent-child relationship had been so close, so concentrated. It may come as a shock to the devoted parents that their only child is developing a life of his own, which they are not being invited to share. They may believe, quite mistakenly, that by making a very normal demand for privacy, their youngster is rejecting them. Parents must realize that the adolescent is developing a concept of himself as an individual. And in order to accomplish this, he must have the privacy in which to experiment with character traits and opinions. He is striving to become a clearly recognizable person who has thought through and worked out his own opinions and his own life-style. This is a formidable goal indeed, one toward which many continue to strive during their adult lives and which many never accomplish.

The need for privacy marks the beginning of the journey to self-realization. True, the adolescent's demands for privacy are sometimes excessive, but adolescence is a period of excesses and of learning controls. The proper role of parents is to anticipate, prepare, set reasonable standards and limits, and accept. Above all, parents must respond intelligently to the normal vagaries of adolescence, providing understanding and support for the young person during this difficult and crucial time.

INDEPENDENT DECISION-MAKING

Decision-making is another common area of conflict between the adolescent only child and his parents. In a family where there are several children, many demands are made on the time and energy of the parents. Some decision-making is, of necessity, left to the individual children. Each youngster quickly learns that he will have to decide for himself how to deal with most minor, everyday problems. The older children often act as advisors to their younger sisters and brothers in reaching decisions. Or a child may seek the advice of his peer group. These children generally take only major problems to their busy parents. Consequently, in a multiple-child family, there is less likelihood of conflict between parents and adolescent over the young person's need to make his own decisions.

Matters are quite different in the single-child family. The parents have all the time they need to concentrate on every dilemma that faces their child, no matter how insignificant. All too often, these intensely involved parents make all the child's decisions for him. Consequently, the adolescent only child may have to wage a tremendous fight to take control of the decision-making process in his daily life. Often, the parents of an only child are unprepared for their youngster's efforts to reach his own decisions. They are alarmed when he does not turn to them for guidance. The prospect that the young person's decision may differ from the one they would reach may be extremely frightening to overprotective parents. Most of all, they may have little faith in the adolescent's ability to assess a situation and reach a sensible conclusion by himself.

It is vitally important for the parents of an only child to recognize that their youngster must develop confidence in his ability to make his own decisions and that he must also learn to live with the consequences of his decisions. Along the way, the young person will make some poor decisions and consequently undertake some unproductive activities, but he will learn from his mistakes and profit from his losses. Parents must not give way to the impulse to protect their only child from life's misadventures and painful experiences, either by preventing experimentation or by warning him of every possible hazard. Such actions, although well-intentioned, will be regarded by the adolescent as dictatorial and will only serve to whet his appetite and challenge him to rebel. This is not to diminish the importance of intelligent parental guidance, but the young adult must assume the ultimate responsibility for his own actions and decisions. Wise parents will permit their only child to begin to participate in the decision-making process soon after he has reached the age of four or five. The young person who has been given some measure of independence since early childhood and who knows that his parents will provide intelligent guidance and support if he requests it is likely to experiment only in ways that are positive and creative.

EXPRESSING INDEPENDENT OPINIONS

Part of the adolescent's search for an individual identity is experimentation with opinions that are very different from those of his parents. The experience of expressing a differing opinion and of having it receive serious consideration by others is a crucial step in the direction of self-realization. All adolescents fling differing opinions at their parents, but the only child will often do so with special intensity. All his life, he has listened to the opinions of his parents and of their friends and colleagues. Because of the tendency to form close individual friendships rather than group friendships, he is not likely to have been exposed to a variety of youthful opinions. The adults who make up the only child's immediate world may have shown little interest in the youngster's opinions. Indeed, they may never have stopped to consider the possibility that he might have ideas which are not in perfect harmony with their own. Then, inevitably, the adolescent bursts forth with the years of stored-up opinions, and his parents are startled and confused because so many of the ideas are very different from their own. Conservative parents are alarmed to hear their son or daughter express extremely liberal views. Religious parents are shocked when their adolescent child denounces religion as hypocritical and a barrier to social progress.

How should parents respond? By understanding that the young adult is testing his wings, listening to himself as he speaks, learning, and developing a set of ideas and beliefs. Ultimately, these beliefs may not differ too radically from those of his parents, but the potential for difference exists and must be recognized. Parents must realize that the objective of parenting is the creation of an independent individual, not a mirror image of themselves. Just as we teach our children tolerance and acceptance of the normal variations within mankind, we must extend that understanding to our children themselves. It is far better to have an only child who holds divergent opinions but who is proud and constructive in applying his thoughts than to have an only child who mouths his parents' words and never has an original thought. We rear our children not to repeat our opinions, but to act as agents of constructive change in the world.

ROLE MODELS

All adolescents go through some predictable shifts in loyalty to their parents. During very early adolescence, the young person will shift his attention from the parent of the opposite sex to the parent of the same sex. Then there will be an emphatic rejection of the parent of the same sex, and the teen-ager will make minimal Oedipal overtures to the parent of the opposite sex. These are common phases in the maturational process, and they are essentially the same for both boys and girls. Parents with several children learn to anticipate and to accept these sudden changes in allegiance. But the parents of an only child may experience considerable anxiety over these sudden shifts.

However, if the parents understand what this behavior means, they will quickly realize that they have nothing to fear. In early adolescence, the youngster moves toward the parent of the same sex for modeling purposes, that is, to emulate and develop the characteristics of adult sexual identity. Once this identity is secure, the young person is ready to stand on his own. In order to achieve this independence, the adolescent will turn away from the parent. Once the adolescent has found his own identity, he will be ready to reaffirm his membership in the family unit. He will be able to accept his parents as adults with whom he shares love and affection. It requires two fully realized adults to negotiate and create a successful, communicative, loving relationship. This is the kind of adult the adolescent is seeking to become; he must be given every opportunity to do so.

It is not uncommon for parents of an only child who is going through the normal adolescent rebelliousness and withdrawal to complain that they are no longer needed. Such parents interpret their youngster's growing independence as a rejection; they may feel that they have failed as parents. This is wrong indeed. The true goal of child-rearing is to raise a child so that one day early in his adult life he will be able to leave the family nest and manage successfully on his own. It is as simple as that.

16

The Adopted Only Child

AT ONE TIME, MANY SOCIAL agencies had an unwritten law that a couple who adopted one child should be strongly encouraged to adopt a second in order to protect the first from being an only child. Today, the situation has changed dramatically. Fewer infants are available for adoption because both contraceptives and abortions are more accessible. This makes a second adoption more difficult and more unlikely. Therefore, many families that adopt one child will end up rearing an only child by default. But there are also many couples who prefer to raise only one child. Consequently, the adopted only child is no longer a rarity.

SPECIAL HAZARDS FOR PARENTS

Adoption is usually undertaken only after a couple has made numerous unsuccessful attempts to have a child. This often means long years of planning and fantasizing. Consequently, when a child is finally adopted, the enthusiastic parents may go overboard, breaking every child-rearing rule in an effort to please their youngster. The problems and the potential hazards parents are likely to face in raising an only child are greatly magnified if that child is adopted. Adoptive parents often feel they must prove to their child that they are worthy to be his parents. There is usually a substantial time lag between placement of the child and completion of the legal adoption procedures. Is it any wonder, then, that parents of an adopted child may be overly sensitive to the child's needs and wishes or that they may encourage excessive dependency as a reassuring sign that the child belongs to them?

Adoptive parents need careful and thorough guidance both before the adoption and after the child has entered their home. Continued counseling will help the parents to maintain their sense of proportion in spite of the highly charged emotions that often surround adoption.

DISCIPLINE

There is a natural tendency on the part of adoptive parents to want to ensure their child's love. They may believe the popular myth that natural parenthood guarantees automatic love between parents and child. But the newborn infant loves no one. He or she will respond to warmth and caring whether it comes from a stranger or a parent. A newborn is a reflexive being at first. He needs food, warmth, body care, and fondling. It's the giving that matters to him, not the giver. However, adoptive parents are likely to be especially anxious to secure the love of their child. They may try to accomplish this by giving in to every one of the infant's whims, believing that if they deny the adopted child anything, they risk losing his love. Consequently, all attempts at discipline may be abandoned, and the child may be allowed to grow in a totally permissive, unstructured environment.

Adoptive parents must realize that love is earned. The development of respect for the parent as a person, advisor, and disciplinarian is the beginning of a child's lasting love. Parents must not try to cajole or pamper their youngster into loving them. Nor must they try to buy or beg for his love. If the child is given a properly structured upbringing, with affection, care, support, attention, and concern for him as a person, love will grow naturally.

DOMINANCY

The loving overindulgence of the adopted only child may not stop in infancy; it may continue as the child grows. As the years go by, the child's every demand is attended to, and the inevitable result is his total domination of his parents. This may seem a happy circumstance to the child because he will get whatever he wants, but in reality the drawbacks are cumulative and serious. He will ultimately lose more than he gains. Whom will he turn to in a time of crisis if his parents have become his slaves? Can he respect two adults who have allowed themselves to be ruled by his domineering behavior? Who will guide him over the rough spots in life? Certainly not these two quaking individuals.

DEPENDENCE

The unhealthy dependency that often develops between the only child and his parents may actually be encouraged and cultivated by adoptive parents. They may feel that the more dependent the adopted child is, the more secure their relationship will be. This constitutes an irrational search to validate the parent-child relationship, to make it more "natural." The adoptive parents must be made to realize that overdependency is unhealthy and ultimately destructive.

CAREER AMBITIONS

Parents often have fixed, predetermined career goals for their adopted child even before they bring him home. But such fantasies have been nurtured in the absence of knowledge of the child's intelligence, potential, preferences, and ambitions. Because genetic factors are unknown (and in some cases they *do* play a decisive role), parents may feel that they are obligated to mold the adopted child by creating the environment most conducive to realizing *their* ambitions for the youngster. Such efforts must be avoided. Adoptive parents, like natural parents, must wait and watch for signs of the child's interests, his levels of competence and skill, and his drives and aspirations. Only then should *any* parents assist their child in finding the best way to achieve his ambitions. There is a further reason for adoptive parents to refrain from any attempt to impose their dreams on their child: the adopted only child may deny his own wishes and make every effort to fulfill those of his parents in order to win the adult approval he craves.

EXPLAINING ADOPTION

There is much controversy over whether an adopted only child should be told that he is adopted. My own feeling is that the child should be told. The wish to conceal from the child the fact that he is adopted may signify a sense of shame or embarrassment over the whole process of adoption. Parents may fear that an adopted child feels less loved, needed, or secure; or they may believe that the child will become obsessed with fantasies about his natural parents and spend years searching for them. The parents must not succumb to such fears. A mature parental attitude toward adoption is vital to the happiness and well-being of parents *and* child. If the adoptive parents can honestly and happily accept the idea of giving and sharing and growing together, then they will want their child to understand the special nature of their family.

A child should be told that he is adopted at the earliest possible moment. The fact of adoption should be a normal, fully integrated part of the child's life. Of course, an infant cannot understand what adoption means. Nevertheless, the parents should make the word a part of their everyday conversation with the child. The words *adoption* and *adopted* should be used in combination with words that have positive, happy significance (such as wonderful, loved, special). If the child is surrounded by an atmosphere in which adoption is equated with joy and fulfillment, he will have little difficulty accepting the facts when he is old enough to understand them fully.

As the child grows older, he will begin to ask for some clearer definitions of the term. Parents should then explain the difference between natural birth and adoption, emphasizing the idea that adoption means *choice* and the fulfillment of mutual special needs. They should attempt to answer each of the child's questions about adoption honestly and in the most positive way. They should always indicate the special meaning adoption has for them. The realization that adoption has made possible an enriched family life for parents and child will do much to dispel any anxiety the child may feel.

In some states, school registration forms still ask whether a child is adopted. I strongly object to this practice. What possible significance does this information have for the school system or the teacher? The question suggests that adoption is somehow an abnormal state and that trouble must be constantly watched for by outsiders. Adoption is a private affair, to be shared at the discretion of the people most closely involved, the parents and the child.

Withholding information about a child's adoption is dangerous. When the child *does* find out the fact of adoption was kept secret, he is likely to feel considerable anxiety about both the meaning of adoption and the need for secrecy. He may wonder how this mysterious process has affected the quality of his relationship with his parents. In such cases, the

child often learns the truth during the pre-adolescent or adolescent years, that is, at the time when the need to rebel and
to reject is so essential if the child is to become a mature
adult. A serious split between parents and child is likely to
occur, triggered by the sudden loss of trust in the parents'
honesty.

One of my patients, a twelve-year-old only child, discovered, through an overheard family conversation, that she was
adopted. Her behavior in acting out her anger and pain was
extreme, resulting in an unwanted pregnancy, an abortion,
and ultimately, flight from home into an early, apparently
doomed marriage. She rejected my attempts to help her because she believed that I was a part of the scheme to conceal
the truth, although in fact I had repeatedly encouraged her
parents to tell her at an early age. Her parents continued to
deny the truth, even after she confronted them with it. This
seriously disturbed young girl had to get the facts from other
relatives and from the courthouse. Her loss of faith and trust
in her parents culminated in extreme rejection of them. She
indicated that she felt she had lost her parents, that they had
died. By subsequently acting out their fears, she was inflicting
a devastating punishment. In the end, of course, it was the
girl, not her parents, who suffered the most.

A healthy attitude toward adoption is revealed in a story
told to me recently. Allison's mother had told her that she
was adopted when she was six months old. Not long ago, the
woman received a call from the child's fourth-grade teacher.
"Mrs. P.," the teacher began, "I am having a problem with
Allison. If one child says he has something, Allison always responds by saying, 'Me, too.'" Knowing that her child did
have a great deal in the way of material things, the mother
waited patiently for the rest of the story. "Well, today, we
were reading a story about an adopted child. Jeremy, who is
adopted, stood up and announced that he was adopted and
told us all about it. Then, Allison stood up and said, 'Me,
too.' Now, don't you think this has become serious enough
for you to have a talk with her?" The teacher was startled as
she heard the mother begin to chuckle. When Mrs. P. stopped
laughing, she said quietly, "But you see, Allison is adopted.
She's known since she was six months old. Just what would
you like me to say to her?" The teacher was silent for a moment; then she whispered, "Oh, I didn't know." Mrs. P. re-

sponded quickly: "There was no reason for you to know until Allison wanted you to. Obviously she does now. Thank you for calling." The conversation ended. Apparently, the only person uncomfortable about Allison's adoption was her teacher.

17

Two Only Children in One Family

IF A FAIRLY LONG PERIOD OF time (eight years or more) elapses between the births of the first and second child, there is a chance that a couple will, in effect, raise two only children. The situation is by no means unusual. However, there is nothing wrong in being two happy, well-adjusted only children. But they will miss a unique experience: the pleasures of the competition and conflicts that inevitably occur between siblings who are close in age.

Clearly, a thirteen-year-old boy and a three-year-old girl or a fourteen-year-old girl and a two-year-old boy will have little in common. The parents will most likely be occupied with the separate and very different age-related activities of each child. There may be little time for family activities that will create a sense of sharing, a feeling of unity. Therefore, it is important that the parents of two children far apart in age make a special effort to create a sense of family. This will require careful, sensitive planning. Activities in which both children can participate and through which they can relate to each other are essential. At first, that relationship may be rather remote, but the foundation will have been established. Then, as time minimizes the age differential between the siblings, their relationship will grow and deepen, enriching their lives.

INVOLVING THE OLDER CHILD

The older child should be actively involved in the planning and preparations for the new baby as soon as possible. The youngster should be told of the pregnancy in the most positive terms, and easy, open discussions of the stages of pregnancy should be encouraged. The growth of an unborn child is indeed a miracle, and the older child should share in this wonder. (This is also excellent sex education for a preadolescent youngster.) In addition, the older child can help to prepare a room for the new baby and assist his parents with household chores. The goal of these efforts is a happy, interested, involved older child who will welcome his new sibling.

After Drew was born, his parents tried for many years to have another child but were unsuccessful. Drew and his parents had a good and loving relationship, but he was beginning to resent their intense concern about his everyday activities and achievements. On several occasions, he behaved aggressively in school; it was as if he wanted to punish his overprotective parents. At fourteen, Drew was healthy and strong but unsettled. His communication with his father was minimal, and he resented his mother because he believed that she had set standards and expectations that he would never be able to satisfy. He was rapidly approaching the crisis of adolescent rebellion, a crisis intensified by his onliness.

About this time, Drew's mother discovered that she was pregnant. She and her husband came to see me at my office. We discussed involving Drew in the preparations for the birth of the baby, and we concluded that it would be wise to treat him as an adult. Drew was astonished by the news. To sustain his adolescent anger, he had come to view his parents as positively senescent; now, he had to make a more realistic evaluation of them. His father requested Drew's help in building some baby furniture, converting a den into a room for the baby, and sharing some of the household chores as the months of pregnancy made his mother less agile. Drew responded cautiously. He went along with his father to purchase paint and lumber, and he asked if he could try building a toy box by himself. His father agreed but asked that Drew also share in the painting chores. As their work progressed, Drew gradually began to open up and talk with his father. He asked questions, sought advice, and talked about his growing excitement over the baby's arrival. His father responded gently, offering advice but never exceeding the limits of the questions. Soon, Drew was talking freely about his worries about peer relationships and his feelings of being unable to live up to the standards he believed his parents had set for him. Drew's father responded simply; he reviewed, analyzed, repeated Drew's words, and pointed out alternatives.

third parent. Either intentionally or unintentionally, he may But he never offered solutions. Gradually, Drew began to realize that he could resolve his problems himself. Throughout her pregnancy, Drew's mother explained the stages of the baby's growth and shared with him the first stirrings of life within her. Drew responded with great interest and concern. By the time Drew's sister was born, the family was able to rejoice in two other births: the birth of a new, more mature relationship between parents and child and the birth of Drew's clear sense of identity.

SHARING RESPONSIBILITY

The older child should be encouraged to share in the day-to-day responsibilities of caring for his new sibling. Such direct involvement will help to strengthen the older child's commitment and will provide a very tangible expression of caring and affection. It is also superb training for eventual parenthood. As the younger child grows, the older sibling can introduce the games, books, and pleasures he himself has enjoyed, thus enriching the youngster's life and expanding his experience of the world.

There is a danger that the older child may attempt to assume too much responsibility. Because of the substantial difference in age, he may view himself, not as a sibling, but as a attempt to take control of the youngster's upbringing. However, his ideas about child-rearing methods will almost always be the same as his parents', even though he may not recognize them as such. Ironically, if a rebellious older child takes on the role of surrogate parent because he is dissatisfied with the way he himself was raised, he is likely to repeat the very practices of which he so strongly disapproves. The greatest danger of such a power struggle between parents and older child is that it will create anxiety and serious confusion in the mind of the younger child.

This problem can be avoided if the parents and their older child arrive at a clear understanding of each other's roles before the birth of the second child. Rules and responsibilities should be established and adhered to. Lines of authority must be understood and respected. Consistency is essential to the successful rearing of a child, whether it is the first child or the second.

OLDER CHILD AS A ROLE MODEL

Inevitably, the young child will look upon his older sister or brother (as well as the parent of the same sex) as a role model. In fact, he may feel closer to his sibling than to his parents when it comes to questions of behavior or life-style. This may become a serious problem for the older child. He may find that the youngster is constantly around him, watching him and asking to be included in his activities, often inappropriately. The young child may even go into the older sibling's room when he is not there and try on his clothes or read his personal papers and books.

Parents must be aware of this possibility and be careful to protect the privacy of the older child. The relationship between the two children will be in serious jeopardy if the older child's rights as an individual are not respected. And in this matter, he will need the firm support and sensitive intervention of his parents.

A great deal of work will be necessary to bridge the gap between two children who are widely separated in age, but parents will find that the effort is deeply rewarding. Before the birth of the second child, they should take all the time they need to review and analyze their experiences in rearing their first child. What were the problems, the mistakes, the successes? This is not to suggest that the older child may not be perfectly happy and well adjusted. But, quite simply, the parents will have benefited from their years of child-rearing experience. They will be able to bring greater awareness and maturity to the job of being parents for a second time.

18

Divorce and the Only Child

DIVORCE STRIKES THE FAMILY UNIT like lightning, shattering the solid family foundation upon which children have based their daily existence. Often the decision is sudden, creating in the children a shocklike state of disbelief. At other times, the process of dissolution is slow and painful. Arguments and disagreements increase in intensity. Silences express anger and regret. The times of easy laughter and shared pleasure are over. One would almost suspect that the child who lives through the daily decay of his parents' relationship would almost hope for the quick and merciful ending and resolution of the incompatibility. But it is the rare child who honestly wants the ultimate solution to be divorce. There is a constancy and base for the child in the nuclear family. Therefore, no matter how well prepared he may be for the eventual separation of his parents, the child still wants an intact nuclear family, at any cost. The predictability of the divorce makes the blow and the adjustment no less difficult for the informed, older child than the protected, unsuspecting younger child. The accommodation for all children is a major emotional-social-cultural undertaking at an age when the knowledge necessary to make such adjustments has not been tested or sampled in any previous experience.

It becomes extremely important to discuss at length the impact of divorce on the only child because of the significant percentages of marriages which often end early and not infrequently after the birth of but one child. Thus the only child may face the immediacy of divorce at a very young age if the child was an early arrival within a shaky marriage. Or he may be forced to cope with divorce at an older age if the parents grow apart and decide against having more children.

In addition, the one-child family often contains "convincers" of the practicality of separation and divorce. The parents are often both career-oriented. The fact that the divorce will effect but a single child may motivate them to consider separation more readily than if a multiple family of growing children were involved. The fact that the single child has reached the "age of reason" may precipitate one or both parents to rend a marriage which has been tolerated due to a sense of responsibility toward and interdependency with the younger only child. The "grown" child is perceived incorrectly as more capable of handling the dissolution of the integral family constellation. Often the moment chosen by such insensitive but stressed parents who have been "waiting for the right time" is during the preadolescent or early adolescent period when the nuclear family structure becomes so vital to the child, though not as visibly as when the child was younger.

There is no correct time for a divorce. I do not condemn divorce because for many marriages, the only sane and rational solution to the mutually incompatible problems is separation. However, the timing should depend much more upon the tensions and communication gaps which are growing between the parents than on the age of children, particularly on the age of an only child. To subject an only child to the hellish years of an acrimonious and bitter marriage, peppered with recriminations and angry outbursts, is poor training indeed for future relationships. If a marriage is obviously not going to last and grow into a mutually rich and productive relationship, then the parents of the only child should wisely counsel each other or seek outside advice to reach the rational decision to end the marriage at the appropriate time in their own lives. If the parents have waited nobly (and often unwisely) to "see the only child through the important years," then they should carry this decision to the most reasonable conclusion and attempt to maintain a contained and comfortably negotiated relationship until the child is independent and capable of functioning on his own.

Very often, the parents note that the adolescent is away from home a great deal, relates only superficially with either of them and then often negatively. This is mistakenly interpreted by parents as the appropriate time for splitting the marriage foundation. It is this foundation against which the young adult is rebelling. It is this foundation which permits experimentation with new ideas, life-styles, viewpoints. Having the family to return to when and if desired is the "catcher in the rye." Thus the destruction of the family structure, no matter how insignificant it may seem to the adolescent, will remove the supports around which he is constructing his own specific individualized house of personal identity. Without parental role models to explore, evaluate, use, or discard, the teen-ager must seek outside figures to formulate or reject. Thus divorce during the key adolescent period is not as benign as it might appear on the surface, particularly for the only child who has no other sibling to fall back upon.

Divorce is almost like death—a loss has been suffered, a separation has taken place, a former stable situation will no longer exist. And the only child faces the separation by himself. Therefore it becomes essential to evaluate what the child might be experiencing, what thoughts and feelings might be pushing to the surface, what the parents might do to soften the stinging blow.

The immediate, very real response of the only child is the sense of loss. One parent will usually move out, or both may move away from the child on a temporary basis, leaving the child with a relative or caretaker. Whatever the situation, the child will feel that the parent or parents are, in fact, divorcing the child. Careful discussion, preferably with both parents present, should focus upon the fact that it is indeed the two adults who are moving apart, away from each other; but, in no way, are they moving away from the child. There should also be an honest attempt to reassure the only child that there still may be shared experiences, if only those related to special occasions. No matter how angry one or both of the adults involved in the action of separation and divorce become, this anger and diffused negativism must not be allowed to spill over onto the only child and stain the internal fabric of his life. Making the only child understand that the separation has not changed the feelings or the attitudes of each parent toward him is of paramount importance. The need for this reassurance when the only child faces divorce begins at about the age of four or five years of age and continues throughout the adolescent period. The words may be different, the interactions and reactions more or less sophisticated and probing, but the essential fact that the parental separation does not mean loss of one or both parents is the basic fact which must be transmitted quickly and as assuredly as possible to the only child of any age.

One emotional reaction of children to divorce is an over-whelming sense of guilt. The guilt is rarely that the child has precipitated or caused the divorce but that he has either been oblivious to the impending crisis, or, even if aware, has been powerless to stop the family disruption from occurring. The sense of the failed crusader lingers heavily on the shoulders of the only child whose parents have told him that they are divorcing. At times, the very young child equates his own misdemeanors and misbehavior with the sudden change in his parents' relationship. This distortion of cause and effect will precipitate a great deal of self-flagellation and fear of action and reaction within the child. The divorcing parents must watch for sudden withdrawal, negative behavior, and seeming disinterest in the surrounding world by the previously active, alert, positive only child. The sense that the young child has of being "punished" for previous behavior patterns by the parents' separation may well result in serious social withdrawal.

Only children who sense impending marital crisis within their family structure may put forth great efforts to abort any disruption or imagined separation. I had as a patient a twelve-year-old girl who appeared in my office with severe headaches and fainting spells. She was worked up thoroughly for these worrisome symptoms, but all of the tests came back normal in all respects. She continued, however, to black out in school and at home. Her headaches kept her in bed on numerous occasions. Before subjecting her to a series of very extensive and intricate neurosurgical examinations, I decided to attempt some in-depth interviewing of parents and child. The parents were in their late thirties, both extremely attractive, dynamic career people who lived a highly charged, volatile existence which took them away from home a great deal. They had been separated much of the time during the preceding year and had begun to draw apart during recent months—one into an extramarital affair, the other into the upward mobility of a potentially important and lucrative career. They had not given serious thought to separation or divorce, although as we spoke, they realized how dangerously close they were to it. However, their twelve-year-old daughter was acutely and painfully aware of the changes that were occurring in her family. She wanted desperately to hold these two people together, fasten their relationship as tightly as possible by the only means she had—herself. As the parents talked, they revealed that the girl, as a young child, had had eczema, which required much parental attention as to diet and skin care. They had shared the responsibilities and had watched the skin problem finally subside when she was seven years old. This background of illness had given her the basis to attempt a form of manipulative behavior over her parents' marriage. My interviews with the girl did not reveal a willingness to share her manipulative behavior with me. I suspected that her symptoms were well up within her conscious level of thinking, but she was extremely fearful that the exposure of her attempts at feigning illness would allow her parents to divert their combined attention from her and toward the shambles she had correctly perceived they had made of their marriage. I advised the parents to attempt— slowly, subtly, but progressively—reassuring the girl that the marriage was stable, that it would survive the intercurrent maladjustments and interferences. The parents decided to begin marriage counseling on a regular basis. The marriage held up rather well under the strain of analysis and readjustment. Within six months, all of the young girl's symptoms had disappeared. She had become a malingerer to keep her parents together; the feigned illnesses were no longer necessary once she truly believed that the marriage was on a solid, continuous grounding.

After divorce, the only child may feign illness or symptoms in an effort to reunite the parents or to bring the two warring parents back within the same orbit—that of their stricken child. If the divorced parents are faced with a child who is using symptoms of ill health or emotional problems manipulatively, it becomes their responsibility to reevaluate their relationships with their child and what these feigned illnesses are suggesting. Most commonly, the child is begging for a rational approach to child care by the divorced parents in a common, uniform, mutually caring, supportive manner.

When parents separate, the child's sense of internal security caves in. The stable feeling of belonging to an intact family unit is pulled out from under the child. However, when one is within a multiple-child family, there remains the inevitable security of the banding together and continuity of the sibling interrelationships. Unlike the child from the large family, the only child does not have the ability to withdraw into the warm, protective confines of the multiple-sibling environment. The security of belonging no longer exists. One cannot belong when there is nothing to belong to. The heightened sense of insecurity—immediate and long-range—is natural. "What is going to happen to me?" is the question that immediately crosses the only child's mind. And with both parents very self-involved in the intricate emotional and legal tangles, the only child will also wonder on repeated occasions, "Who will be there when I am in need? Who do I turn to?" Neither parent at the time of divorce appears capable of functioning as a strong protective guiding force; their energies are intensely directed elsewhere. The only child consequently feels adrift. Without the protections of the multiple-sibling family, the only child may think of himself as neglected and overlooked during the pre- and post-divorce periods. The feeling of insecurity is justly felt. The key to preventing insecurity is the creation of a defined and structured life pattern—for the present and future—which the only child can understand and accept. Discussion of the separation should include plans relative to how and when the child is to be with each parent as well as the realistic inclusion of the child in the decision-making process of who will be responsible for what and who can be relied upon in each defined situation. There are no set rules; nothing in the developmental manuals has stressed that mothers are appropriate for all types of emotional and educational problems while fathers ought to fulfill disciplinarian roles. If the child is a young adult, he should have some choice in selecting the bearers of different responsibilities in his own upbringing. A solidly constructed set of parental roles based upon the realistic qualities and qualifications of the parents will dispel a fair amount of the insecurity that befalls the only child who sees his internal world visibly crumbling around him.

The game of "loyalties" is too often foisted upon the only child early in the process of divorce. Because of their own inherent sense of guilt and concern, the parents will attempt to explain "their side of the story." This places the child in the position of listening to the regurgitation of the unhealthy aspects of his parents' marriage with the inherent accusations and unspoken resentments. Each parent will retell the story from his or her viewpoint, expecting the child to "understand." In essence, the parent is seeking the approval which will allow freedom from embarrassment in future dealings with the child. I have known divorcing parents attempt to "tell" a child of five what caused the disruption of their marriage. This may seem too foolish to believe, but these parents were desperately vying for the love and affection of their child and needed forgiveness and understanding.

It is not necessary for either parent to be "right" when there is a divorce. They do not need their child's approval of their actions. What they do need is his understanding of his continued unchanging role in their individual lives. Divorcing parents must be very careful not to put the only child in the position of having to decide who is and was right regarding the divorce and the post-divorce process. If they are not careful, the child will be left thinking they were both quite wrong. Parental demands for loyalty may cause the child to simply "turn off" both parents in the process and withdraw from any real, meaningful relationship with either.

When there is only one child over whom the games of favoritism and vengeance can be played, that child is in greater danger of being used as a pawn in the serious game of competitive parentship. No material purchase is too great to win favor; no trip too expensive or extensive to rule out. Arguments over who will buy or do or accomplish permeate the child's existence. He soon learns to manipulate one parent against the other, demanding from one by hinting at the accomplishments, purchases, promises of the other. The parent foolishly sees himself losing a battle—a battle for the attention and affection of the youngster. What every child needs is the strength of parental decision-making which requires discipline and regulatory patterns. If both adults are so busy competing to gain the upper hand in the child's affections, they may be ultimately shocked to discover how little respect their only child has for either of them, how little regard he has for discipline and rules, and how little progress has been made in their child's emotional growth. Competitive games can destroy discipline, rule-setting, and consistent, mutually agreed upon parental regulations; without these constants an only child's ability to mature may be impaired.

A couple separated somewhat unexpectedly and abruptly, in the eyes of their friends and their only son. In truth, their marriage had been deteriorating for years. To the wife, there was "no problem." To the husband, he was "waiting it out." He did just that, to leave his wife suddenly, just before his son's sixteenth birthday. The boy was stunned and crushed.

He immediately resented the failure of the father and mother to give him any previous indication of a continuing family crisis. At first, his mother became reclusive and depressed. The son tried to help but was powerless. His father drifted, seemingly happy at his sudden release from a burdensome marriage. This infuriated the young son. How could his father be so calm and contented when he was left alone with this withdrawn, mourning, depressed woman? He attempted avoiding the situation; but his mother invariably called him back home to attend to her needs or wishes. He was slowly being drawn into the net of replacement, finding himself companion and supporter to his mother while his father remained fancy-free. The young man had difficulty in sensing the subtlety of his mother's gradual transference of the masculine responsibility within the home onto him. He believed, because he was being told to believe, that he was only experiencing the same pain and depression that the mother was experiencing. What was intimated was that his father was primarily to blame, and so he literally excluded his father from his life. But the increasing weight of his mother's dependency and need for constant reinforcement was becoming incompatible with the demands of his teen-age life. Finally one day, he called a close friend of the family, a woman who had been friendly and supportive during past problems, and asked plaintively if she would please call his mother, take her out, get her out of her depression, "save her life." What this young man was begging for was release from the responsibility thrust upon him. The woman responded to the young boy's request only to be turned down by the "mourning" woman. She indicated that she had other plans. Her plans were "dinner with her son."

What can you advise a young man who suddenly finds himself playing the dual role of son and husband because he is an only child of divorced parents? Obviously his mother was unwilling to look at her own behavior. His father had little influence because of the distinct sense of alienation. I advised the boy to get involved in extracurricular activities at school as much as possible. In addition, I suggested that he investigate graduating from his high school early, since he had extra credits and was quite intelligent. This would permit him to go away to college a year earlier and escape the difficulty of playing the unfair role of son and protector for which he was neither emotionally nor experientially prepared.

All too often, the only child of divorcing parents finds himself in the position of assuming extra responsibilities, extra duties, extra emotional burdens which are inappropriate and damaging to his emotional growth. The parents must simply be very careful to avoid transferring roles onto the shoulders of the only child during this stressful and ego-damaging period.

Very often, after the divorce, the only child and his or her mother will develop an even more intensified, tight relationship than existed previously. This should be avoided if at all possible. After a time, the mother will begin to reenter the social arena, begin dating again, and introduce new men into the home. If the prior mother-child relationship has been allowed to become too close and exclusive, the problem of the mother's social life becomes a major concern. The only child may feel deeply threatened by the intrusion of a stranger into a relationship which has recently become more intense and important to him than ever. The only children of divorced parents must be informed and shown as early as possible after the divorce that the private and social existence of the parents will not disappear, that in fact it may intensify. This will prepare the only child for the prospect of parental dating, introduction of new people into the internal circle of his life, and the ultimate possibility of remarriage by one or both parents. The parents, by not depending on the only child to provide the bulk of companionship and by going out in groups or singly as soon as possible after the separation, will show the child the continuing intention of each parent to lead a productive and fulfilling life. There should be no reason for competition between the only child and the parents' social and private lives.

Occasionally, remarriage will bring an only child into a multiple-child family. The parent must bear in mind that this will require a great deal of adaptation by the only child. One does not change patterns of reaction and behavior overnight. Being in the spotlight, the easy parental accessibility, the noncompetitive only-child-oriented household, the minimal need for sharing—all these are lost as two families come together and the child suddenly has siblings. Jealousies, withdrawal temper tantrums, overall negative behavior may well be the general response if the remarrying parent has not taken the time to orient the only child. Frequent visits to the new family before the marriage, overnight stays, visits from child members of the other family will gradually help the only child adjust. The one real danger in this process is the parent who continues to treat the only child with special consideration after the marriage has taken place. This creates multiple problems. The other children become resentful, which only reinforces any existent negative behavior in the only child. This represents a distinct loss to both the child and to the parent of the only child. The only child will miss the opportunity of an instant multiple family; the parent will alienate the step-children, jeopardize the new marriage, and miss the chance of assimilating two families under the warm and understanding tutelage of new parents.

So often the loser in the game of divorce is the child. The child who has the most to lose and who exists in the most precarious position is the only child. He has no forest of siblings into which he can run and hide. He must confront the immediate and long-range effects of parental divorce squarely and alone. Perceptive and sensitive parents will refuse to allow personal pain and mutual differences to affect their only child and will try to avoid inflicting lifetime wounds.

19

Death of a Parent of
the Only Child

THE LOSS OF A PARENT IS AN agonizing experience for any
child. For the only child, the anguish is intensified because
there are no sisters and brothers to turn to for comfort and
for strength. The problems that any child faces at this time
are magnified for the only child by his onliness.

ANGER

Generally, the first reaction of a child who has lost a
parent is anger, anger directed at the world in general and at
the people closest to him in particular. I was seventeen; it
was after 2:00 A.M. when I returned home from a date one
warm June night to find that my father had suffered a mas-
sive heart attack. He died on the way to the hospital. My initial response was blind, blistering rage: my mother should
have recognized the symptoms sooner; she should not have
waited so long to call the doctor; the doctor should have
come sooner; the ambulance should have been faster.

Because I had no siblings to express it to, I internalized my
anger, a common reaction for an only child, and a harmful
one. Anger that remains unexpressed and unappeased can
reappear in the form of depression and in aggressive behavior
that affects all areas of the child's life. An older sibling can
listen to a younger child's expressions of rage and help the
youngster to see the irrationality of his feelings. At the same
time, this sharing will help the older child to come to terms
with his own anger. The only child needs someone to help
him with his irrational but very natural immediate reactions.

133

GUILT

All children feel a sense of guilt when a parent dies. This guilt takes three distinct forms. First, the child feels that somehow he should have been able to prevent the death. In my own case, I was tormented by the conviction that I could have come home earlier, been more effective, somehow done something to save my father's life. The only child has no one with whom to share this sense of responsibility for the loss. Nevertheless, this guilt can be dispelled by sensitive counseling. The child must be helped to understand the inevitability of the parent's death. If the death was not inevitable, the child must be made to realize that he could not have helped because he lacks the necessary professional skills.

Second, the child is overwhelmed by memories of harsh words, arguments, and conflict. The child may long to go back and undo the disagreements, the times when love was temporarily forgotten in the heat of the moment. When there are brothers and sisters experiencing the same feelings and memories because they, too, lived through similar conflicts, the youngster is able to see such past anger in the proper context: as a part of the normal pattern of family living. But the only child has no one with whom to share these feelings. Furthermore, the problem may be magnified because of the special intensity of the relationship between parent and only child. Frequent heated disagreements are not uncommon in the single-child family. Again, the only child needs help in easing his remorse.

Third, the child is tormented by thoughts of what might have been. This is a particularly devastating form of guilt because it focuses on speculations about what never was rather than on the reality of what has been, and it leads only to continued pain. The child is filled with regret for opportunities missed, experiences not shared—for all the things the relationship could have been if it had had the time to grow and deepen. This particular guilt is one I suffered from greatly for many years. I felt responsible for not having brought my relationship with my father to mature fulfillment. I had tried to share his enthusiasm for fishing and other sports but had failed miserably; he had tried to understand my love for the theater, but he, too, had failed. We apparently had nothing in common except an interest in horse-racing. This seemed so little, so empty. It was not until I had children of my own that I understood an essential truth about the parent-child relationship: even the most minor, apparently insignificant contact between parent and child has profound emotional significance. I realized that those days at the racetrack and even those futile attempts to share each other's special interests had been times of real communication and that we could have gone on to create a rich relationship. Death had prevented this flowering, but I understood at last that I had no reason for guilt.

NEED FOR INDEPENDENCE

Very often, as a result of the death of a parent, the only child will suddenly find himself in a position requiring a great deal of independent thought and action. He must cope with the world without the firm support of either parent. The surviving parent may be too incapacitated by grief or too preoccupied with the struggle to support the family to provide advice and instruction normally depended on by the child. And yet the child's life must go on; he must return to school and to the society of other youngsters. But because of the tendency toward a close and dependent relationship between parents and their only child, the youngster may be totally unprepared to assume so much independence. Ideally, the only child should have been taught to be self-reliant while he was still quite young. If this training has been successful, the only child will be stimulated to meet the challenge of this forced independence. But if he has not been adequately prepared for self-sufficiency, he must be helped in this time of crisis. Despite pressures of grief and money, the surviving parent must help the child to gain self-assurance and gradually assume increasing responsibility for himself. Family friends and other respected adults can be of great assistance to the young person as advisors and as behavior models. Without help, such an extremely vulnerable and immature only child will experience serious difficulties in dealing with the outside world, perhaps for the rest of his life.

UNHEALTHY ROLES AND RESPONSIBILITIES

The loss of a parent means a sudden shift in the family structure. When there is more than one child, the children themselves may assume various responsibilities, providing strength and support for each other and for their grieving parent until he or she can take control of the family again. But the only child is the only person to whom the suddenly dependent, mourning parent can turn. The child may find himself child, comforter, and surrogate mate to the surviving parent. Although this is not an uncommon pattern, it should be avoided if at all possible because it will prevent the child from mourning at the appropriate time and in a natural, healthy manner.

It is perfectly normal and acceptable for a daughter or a son to take over some of the household responsibilities of the dead parent. The only child can easily adapt to such changes. But a parent who makes excessive demands on the child to fulfill the companionate and social roles of the dead parent is forcing the child to play a dangerous and unsuitable role: surrogate mate. The child's normal growing up will be distorted by demands for adult behavior for which the child is unprepared. If the only child is a son replacing a dead father or a daughter replacing a dead mother, there are obvious sexual connotations involved. The confusion about the sexual and intellectual responsibilities that the child owes the remaining parent may cause serious damage to the child's chances of developing into a mature adult, both sexually and socially. Every parent of an only child who has lost a partner through death or divorce must remain constantly aware of these dangers and must make certain that the parent-child relationship is not allowed to become pathological.

NEED FOR SUPPORT

Mourning allows the living to come to terms with their grief and their loss. It is an essential therapeutic process. The only child *must* be allowed to mourn: to cry, to withdraw, to act out his grief and pain in any reasonable and healthy way that works for him, no matter how quiet or explosive or foolish. His mourning may be brief or prolonged; it may match or contrast with the manner in which the adults resolve their grief. But it is vital that the only child not be left to mourn alone. He must have support from another person who can help him to understand the experience and his own reactions to it. He needs someone who will listen intelligently, answer questions tactfully, offer warm and loving physical contact when that can ease the pain, and be sensitive to his need for privacy. Because the grief-stricken parent is usually not emotionally able to help the child at this time, someone else must be available to guide him through his mourning. In my experience as a pediatrician, I have seen this task admirably performed by aunts or uncles, cousins, family doctors, clergymen, and older family friends.

An only child runs the risk of losing his identity in the process of adjusting to a parent's death. He will have to be many things and fulfill many responsibilities during this time of great stress, but he must not be prevented from fully resolving his grief. He must go on to build a new and productive life. He cannot do this alone. In all aspects of dealing with death, the child needs the help of a mature and compassionate other person.

20

The Future of
the Only Child:
Career and Marriage

THE ONLY CHILD'S CHOICE OF CAREER CAN often be traced back directly to the special aspects of his upbringing as the singular child. He has frequently been exposed to a wide variety of stimuli which had an impact upon his decision-making and planning. At times, this abundance of experiences creates a problem for the youth in ultimately pinning down a single field of interest to pursue. It is not at all unusual for the only child, who stands at the midcollege or even graduate threshold, to be perplexed and anxious because there are two, three, or sometimes even four interests vying for a permanent commitment from him. Often the person will compromise by selecting one field as a career, maintaining another as a high-priority avocation, and in some cases intermittently delving into a third for occasional entertainment or relaxation. The only child has the capacity of being not only peripatetic but also of remaining at a high stimulation level, not only as a child but also as an adult.

Given that the only child will often substitute fantasy for reality during the younger years as a means of creating companionship within the strange adult world in which so much of his time is spent, is it any wonder that only children would gravitate readily to the fields where fantasy plays the major role? Namely, writing and acting. Having become accustomed to losing oneself in the milieu of the unreal, the outside-of-self world, the imaginary, it is a natural transition to channel this behavior into a creative vein and amplify the pleasurable "other" world for other people. For instance, if one analyzes the publishing and writing fields alone, one would be amazed at the number of only children who have developed their love of books and the written word into positions within the businesses dealing with the creation and production of books, magazines, plays, etc.

Individual sports, such as swimming, and one-to-one sports, such as tennis, attract the only child. The choice of sports as a career would more likely fall in one of these areas than in the collective athletic team sports such as football, baseball, or basketball.

Parents usually set very high standards and have very high expectations for their only child. There may have been overt or subliminal hints as to the area and type of career choice which would best satisfy the family's expectations. Usually, they hope that the child will become a "professional." Because of his strong need for adult approval, the only child may select from a limited number of acceptable "professions" into which he will direct himself. A survey of the applicants to medical, dental, law, and pharmacy schools reveals an extremely high percentage of only children. The problem with this desire to fulfill parental aspirations is that the young person's interest and talent may not lie primarily in any one of these fields. Thus, he is making a lifetime compromise to satisfy his parents' goals for him. How long such a career choice will sustain the only child as an adult will depend upon the rewards he receives from his field and his continuing sense of loyalty to his parents and his belief in their philosophies. Often, the breaking point comes in middle age. Rebellion at that time can be costly and painful. It is far better for the only child to turn his back on the selected profession before or during his training than years later when many more gates have been closed to him.

Interestingly, only children often play "school" and "teacher" either alone or with a single close friend. The ability to interact and, in a sense, dominate in an intellectual way in such school games creates a comfortable play theme. Since educational achievement is one of the parental expectations realized by most only children, playing "school" reinforces the adaptive behavior within the classroom and allows for pleasurable alternative means of extra study and higher grades. The transition from these youthful games to an educational career is therefore quite natural. The behavior and the attitudes have been learned and perfected, while the intellectual environment, which allows for some degree of dominance and control, satisfies the psychological needs of the adult only child.

Control, dominance, central focus, repeated approval, and visible, palpable success seem often to motivate career selections. The only child might also turn to politics as a career. Previous difficulties in adapting to group activities may prove a distinct disadvantage because politics requires constant interaction with individuals, small groups, and large crowds. However, politicians must be very good actors, able to play the roles of friend, participant, interested onlooker, or advisor. The better they play the role, the more votes they will get. Thus, only children, who are usually exceptionally good actors, may be able to bring this skill into the political scene.

Whether the only child will find pleasure or contentment in his chosen career will depend upon how the decision was made. If the decision was his—carefully sifted from the multiple possibilities of a highly stimulated only childhood—then the chances for a high degree of personal satisfaction are very good. If the decision was made by others or to please others, then the possibility of frustration and daily dissatisfaction with the chosen field is very real. Clearly, the only child needs the time to sort out the career choices that his varied life experiences have made possible. He needs to experiment with the various alternatives, and he must feel free to change, to be flexible in his career choices. He must not feel bound to a career that was not chosen by him or not based upon a realistic assessment of his talents or interests. Advice should be offered by parents only if requested. No hidden agendas or unspoken expectations must lurk beneath the benign surface which permits the child's self-selection. Once the career decision is finalized, the parents must take the wise road of complete acceptance, and support all future efforts toward the goal.

The overreaction of the only child to manipulative parents who have selected the future life-style and life's work for their offspring can often result in the child avoiding all of the rational and reasonable career choices in which he has the talent and inclination to succeed. This overly programmed only child will punitively select a life-style and a work program which is diametrically opposite to that desired by his parents and, unfortunately, often quite deviant from his own inherent abilities and interests. He is, in actuality, severely punishing himself through the act of hurting and negating his parents and their overbearing impact upon his life. The parents of the only child must bear this possibility in mind as they begin the subtle manipulations which they hope will direct their only child to the career of *their* choice.

What special qualities does an only child bring to a marriage that should be recognized as having potentially positive or negative influences? The only child's background has, in many ways, been quite divergent from the siblings of a multiple-child family. A full understanding of the potential hurdles and possible benefits by both partners in an only-child marriage might make the first years of the marriage less rocky and more compatible.

One extremely positive aspect of an only child's entering marriage is the well-established tendency of many only children to maintain single friendships for long periods of time, with all of the attendant adjustments and adaptations that each friend has had to make to the other. This can be of great benefit to a successful marriage, which is, I believe, the total realization of a satisfying extended friendship. Once the physical aspect of the marital relationship reaches the normal, settled, comfortable phase, a foundation of mutual concern, sharing, and friendship is necessary to expand and enrich the marriage. Only children who have successfully learned the process of modifying their behavior, adapting their style somewhat, adjusting their needs and wants to accommodate the differences in the friend therefore have an advantage in marriage.

However, only children do tend to develop somewhat dominant personalities because of their ability to control much of their home environment. The only child who has not had this tendency toward dominance broken as a result of group interaction, and remains a controlling, subtly domineering person as a young adult, may have problems in negotiating the proper balance in the marriage situation. In most marriages, one partner must give in to the other on minor and, at times, major points of disagreement or conflict. If the only child demands consistent control, then the other partner will be compromised into constantly relinquishing his or her beliefs to satisfy the need of the only-child partner to be in continuous control, to dominate, to "get his way." This imbalance will survive for only a very brief period. The other person will eventually rebel, demanding to be heard and recognized as a force within the marriage. It will depend upon the flexibility of the only-child partner and his or her ability to modify behavior so as to balance control within the marriage. Otherwise trouble.

Overachievement is characteristic of many only children and the drive for it is far greater than that possessed by the average sibling from a large family. Thus, the only child may be compulsively neat, frugal, or intense about deadlines or work achievements. This can be extremely frustrating to a marital partner if the same behavior is expected of him or her. The only child married to the more relaxed, less self-demanding partner who has the background of a large, heterogenous family may attempt to impose the compulsive rules of high achievement and strict task attainment on the partner only to be amazed and shocked at the intensity of the rebellion that ultimately ensues. Extreme compulsiveness is difficult to live with even if the other person is not expected to follow suit. The only child must continually and carefully assess the rules and demands and structures he or she imposes upon the marriage in order to avoid these patterns.

Sharing is frequently a hard lesson for the only child. But the adult only child usually learns to share the material aspects of the marriage. That adaptation is not an extremely difficult one for the mature person to make. Sharing self may be far more difficult, however, for the only child may be totally unaccustomed to openness and vulnerability, having usually protected himself from the pain of peer rejection. He has learned to release his own feelings and thoughts only after careful assessment of the possible impact upon others. Only children are not, in general, spontaneous people; they are well-defended, guarded against the pain of disapproval and dismissal, whether from one individual or a group. Thus, the only child may have to learn to share feelings, thoughts, and ideas spontaneously and openly with the marriage partner. This will require careful work by the only child and the understanding of the partner until the trust and faith in the other is secure enough to permit the vulnerability of sharing.

What frustrates the mates of many only children is their indecisiveness. Whether an only child brings to marriage the ability to make decisions will largely depend upon the degree to which parents permitted the young person to make his or her own important decisions. If the process of choosing for oneself has been blocked in the past, the only child may actually shy away from family decisions. Or, even more inappropriately, the only child may rely upon his or her parents to continue deciding the questions.

Decision-making in marriage cannot be unilateral. Therefore, the sooner the parents allow their child the freedom to deal with important personal matters, the better prepared the youngster will be for marriage. Dependency proves another stumbling block in many such marriages. The only child, who has been overtly dependent upon the overprotective and overly solicitous parents, may transfer that dependency to the marriage partner who will be expected to carry the entire emotional weight of the other adult. The transference may not occur; and the only child may continue to rely upon the parents for many of the things that are normally the prerogative of the new husband or wife. This weakens the marriage, lessens the potential for the growth of both partners, and diminishes the role of the spouse.

Previous experience may have also taught the only child to believe in the likelihood of expectations being fulfilled. In marriage, this is less likely, compromise being a common necessity. All too often, the only child will be labeled as selfish because of his or her negative reactions whenever a need cannot be fulfilled or a desire is unrealized. Obviously, society will never be able to fulfill all of such a person's whims and wishes. Marriage, then, may be the first area where the only child realizes the degree of accommodation and modification of expectations required for co-existence with others. Parents must help their only child to understand that there are gradations—those that can be realized through the proper effort, those that are unlikely but can be worked for nonetheless, and those that are impossible or impractical and must be dismissed. The only child who has learned this lesson will enter marriage better prepared for the compromises that two people simply must make.

The only child may bring to marriage the need for repeated adult approval, making subtle but definite demands upon the partner for constant reassurances in the areas of love; success as a husband, lover, provider; personal appearance; social behavior among others. The insecurity of previous peer relationships and the subsequent sense of need for adult recognition and approval may leave the imprints of insecurity so vividly on the only child that the marriage takes the form of a continuous, unrelieved psychotherapeutic session in which the only-child partner is consistently being reassured of his competence in all of the daily living areas. No partner can tolerate such demands for very long. The extreme need for constant reassurance and approval may be a key issue in the disruption of an only-child marriage. Parents of the only child must gradually and systematically instill an aura of self-confidence within their only child by pointing up the positive features of his personality and accomplishments and reflecting only minimally and therapeutically upon the negative. This will generate a sense of well-being, strengthen self-concept, and allow the only child to enter marriage, work, and society without the fear that his competence has yet to be tested, that he is still vulnerable to continuous failure.

In reality, the only child can make a superb marriage partner. He may have the previous experience and sensitivity of close singular relationships to build upon. He is usually well-read, has been intensely exposed to the outside world, and is familiar with the adult society in which the marriage game will be played. He is less of a group person and more intensely interested in the other person as a result. The ability to have the other person so close after long years of aloneness often makes the only child an eager, caring, almost overly solicitous mate. There are, however, certain characteristics which must be prevented during the upbringing of the only child if the marriage is to sail smoothly and not founder on the rocks of only-child idiosyncrasies.

The long-range goal of every parent of an only child should be the child's successful adjustment to the world in which he lives as an adult. This social comfort includes any intense adult interrelationship (with marriage as an example), the daily work environment, and should be broad enough to encompass adaptation of the adult only child to the total life situation.

21

The Advantages of Being
an Only Child

FOR YEARS, WHENEVER I WOULD announce under my breath
that I was an only child, I would usually receive a gentle and
soulful glance from my peers or a blatantly pitying look from
the adults that said, "You poor kid." After getting married I
would occasionally remark to our friends that we were both
only children. The responses led us to believe that we were
prime candidates for aid to the disadvantaged. The fact that I
was a pediatrician and my wife worked in early childhood
education at the time somewhat compensated in the eyes of
our friends and associates for the gross deficiencies which we
possessed because of our only-child upbringing. But not quite.
Underneath it all we were really seen as permanent only children, who had compounded the problem by marrying. As I
look back upon my childhood and chat with my wife about
hers, it becomes very obvious that there were aspects to each
of our upbringings that could never have been appreciated
nor achieved by children from large families. Certainly we
had our problem days and months, but we also had positive
periods which were directly attributable to our being only
children.

There *are* advantages growing up in a single-child family,
and no child should have to be ashamed of that. With proper
upbringing that combines parental sensitivity and understanding, the only child need not feel like a social reject, fighting
an uphill battle to establish his emotional and maturational
normality. There are advantages, yet even some professionals
find it difficult to accept the reality that there can be happiness and joy in being a siblingless child. The proper environment can produce a person with very few hang-ups and
many satisfying life experiences.

The only child has a youth period which is free of the often perplexing problem of sibling rivalry. As the second child arrives on the scene, there is a natural tendency for the two to begin vying for the parents' attention and affection. Constant comparisons are unconsciously made in the home in conversation and in action. "Do you remember when Johnny did that?" is a common innocuous comment by the parent at the time of a specific accomplishment by the younger child. Yet the sovereignty of the attainment is lost by one of the siblings, depending on whom the comparison favors. That is, if the second child performs later than had the eldest, the achievement is diminished. Further, the dependency of the younger sibling will often deprive the older child of the attention or concentration of parents during a period when it is much needed. Similarly the resentment of the younger sibling for drawing away the parents' attentiveness at times can become overwhelming and can create a very real block to a healthy future sibling relationship. The only child has none of this—there is no competition for a parent's time, no rivalry for affection. The pressing need to compete is washed away, and the child has the total freedom of establishing a relationship with the adults in his or her life without the accommodations necessary in the multiple-child family.

Additionally, the only child can be himself at all times because of the lack of this internal vying of sibling rivalry. Siblings learn to play games, games which they carve out of the competitive situation, and which they hope will give them the upper hand. Feigned illnesses, school problems, subtle innuendoes about the other's misbehavior, "setting up" the sibling for a parental overreaction—all of these are common ploys in the daily battles that siblings wage for the upper hand. Only children need not resort to these devices for the parental focus they desire. In so many areas, too, the younger child or children in multiple-child families have the heavy burden of the older sibling to live up to. The only child is his own marker. He has no other young people to be compared to or to be assessed against. He is what he is. His level of accomplishments are judged by standards not dictated by other siblings or peers, but created by the potential and effort of the child. These self-created standards should be the criteria for measurement of all children. But they are not. There seems to be a natural tendency to contrast and compare children against the standards of others within the same family rather than by individual accomplishments.

Growing up in a multiple-child family often means the yielding of privacy, while the only child can comfortably have free moments at will. Also, very often in multiple families the children are delegated many responsibilities for the other siblings, while the only child can gradually move toward an increasing degree of self-reliance and independence and self-assurance based upon his ability to focus upon his own maturation and emotional development.

The parents of the only child have that one youngster to concentrate their attentions upon. These attentions include time, affection, and finances. The only child does not have to share these or the parents with another child. A reasonable arrangement will still leave the parents with an abundance of free and open time for themselves. Thus time devoted to their child is not borrowed or robbed from the marriage or from the hours needed by another sibling, but is allotted with the full knowledge that additional time for personal pursuits will be available.

Educationally, the only child also has a decided advantage, given the cost of private schools and colleges. With but one child to educate, the parents have a greater fiscal freedom in selecting public vs. private school and college possibilities, if the young person's academic interest and achievement is sufficient. The only child, therefore, may have educational opportunities not available to his peers. The same is true of extracurricular activities—skiing, gardening, whatever. But even here it is much more likely that the only child will have consistent exposure to the parents' hobbies and avocations than the child with many other siblings. It is not unlikely for the only child to develop the same degree and intensity of interest in the hobby as the parent, because of the pleasure of the exposure, and subsequently follow the parent in the pursuit of the particular avocation as the child matures.

In larger families, the child-oriented ambiance is usually diffuse and directed in multiple channels due to the varying ages of the children. This variability in the children's ages requires the parents to shuttle between the various age periods and the interests intrinsic to each age level. Parents of many children must have considerable adaptive abilities in order to simultaneously satisfy the needs and emotional requirements of the children. The parents of the only child, on the other hand, can be constantly on the same wave length as their child, observing closely, becoming sensitive to changes in the youngster, so that the family unit may shift its interests and activities at the right moment and in the direction of the child's development. The only child's family literally grows up with him or her; each phase, each maturational period, each new venture becomes a joint cooperative experience between the (hopefully) perceptive parents and receptive only child.

The only child rarely has to worry whether the parents will be present at his class play or on the sidelines or in the stands at the important football game. There are seldom other interests which will pull them away. Certainly the simultaneous demands of other siblings will not require their embarrassed absence or the appearance of only one parent as the other parent attempts to fulfill obligations involving the other children.

If a healthy and thoughtful relationship can be established between the only child and his parents, then the only child has the slight edge on his peers because it is probable that a tighter, more cohesive, more intimately interrelated family unit will develop in the three-person family. This can be highly supportive for the only child. What must be remembered is that the line between supportive and suffocating may be subtle; it can be unknowingly crossed. Therefore the relationship should be carefully assessed on a regular basis. Too tight a family structure may impede the emotional growth of the only child; the unity must be firm enough only to act as the roots, the solid foundation, and not the whole life structure and style of the only child.

The multiple-child family can make constant demands upon one or both parents, exhausting and exasperating one or the other at different times. The couple's plans often must be postponed because of the children's demands. This may create a distance, a frustration, an unhappily structured role-playing within the large family which the parents grow to resent. Therefore, unless careful priorities are established within the large family, the children may weaken the marital bonds between the two adults. Anger, resentment, and hostility may be very real and frightening consequences. The only-child family has room within the structure for the marriage to grow along with the rearing of the child. As long as the parents' focus is not solely upon the youngster but is also upon themselves as individuals and their marriage as an ever-changing arrangement, the marriage may be strengthened by the additional time and resources that the parents of a single child can bring to it. This has obvious benefits to the only child.

In many large families, as the younger children push their way up through the ranks, the older children must often assume added responsibility, perform more complex tasks, and make numerous adult decisions. In other words, the child may have to grow up fairly quickly when there are a number of youngsters behind him in age, ready to experience the years through which he has been passing. This early maturation and assumption of responsibility is a common occurrence among the older children in large families, one which is not always healthy for the individual. The only child need not be concerned about such a forced maturation. He is able to grow emotionally at his own rate. There is no one waiting in the wings to go through that phase so that he must move into the next maturational level, possibly earlier and more quickly than he was emotionally ready to do; there are no siblings above or below to block or accelerate emotional growth. Only his parents can force him to slow down or speed up his emotional development. One would hope that this would occur only after serious parental consideration and after professional consultation have indicated that such action is necessary, as for example when a discernible and significant disparity exists between a child's chronological age and his emotional age. Only then should intervention into the only child's progress be made.

Recently I spoke to a young college student who was discussing what it meant to him to have grown up as an only child. He reflected on some of the overdependence and the minimal degree of unwarranted concern his parents evidenced during his earlier years. But he concluded that he had been very contented being "only." When asked why, he smiled, and said very serenely, "I knew that they were always there. They let me be part of them but also be myself. I had nobody to fight with, compete with, or be jealous of. Besides, we did a lot of things together, things that all three of us enjoyed. And they let me go without a hassle. I left for college without tears or sadness because they knew I was coming back. And besides, they were pretty tight, the two of them. I wouldn't mind just having one kid myself if my wife would agree. I didn't mind it at all. In fact, I kinda enjoyed the whole thing."

Being an only child need not be an unhappy experience or one in which the parents or the child feel that they have been deprived. It is merely another alternative style of child-rearing which can be selected by the parents and, if properly handled, can result in a young adult with the same level of emotional growth and maturity as a peer from a large family. Focusing upon the advantages of being an only child and minimizing the disadvantages would appear to be the key.

22

Prescriptions for Raising the Only Child

TO HAVE ONLY ONE CHILD IS A DECISION many young couples are making today. "There is really nothing wrong or abnormal in this choice," I tell such parents. "The choice is yours. And if it's what you want and what you feel will be best for the two of you and your child, then I want it too."

"But, Doctor, we are worried," is the usual response. "We've heard so much about the dangers of being an only child. We've seen a lot of only children who have so many hang-ups and problems. What can we do to prevent this from happening? We want to start now."

PRESCRIPTIONS FOR PARENTS OF THE ONLY CHILD

1. From the moment of birth on, the parents of the only child must be alert to the possibility of overinvesting in various aspects of the child's life, thereby making him quite different from his peer group in the degree of parental involvement. The child will be quick to perceive the excessive emotional dedication of one or both parents. Often this creates in the child a misplaced sense of responsibility—to respond in kind and to attempt to live up to the parent's investment of self. The physical investment includes the actual amount of time and effort focused by one or both parents on the child, as well as the resources (financial and otherwise) which are diverted to the needs and demands of the offspring. Excesses in these areas obviously spoil the youngster and are counter to what the child will soon experience in the outside society, thus creating a dichotomous situation for the child which is frustrating and confusing. It

151

is far too easy for the parent to be caught in the seductive web of "giving all." Don't. Priorities must be chosen. Allowing the infant to cry and wait for feeding a short while until a convenient moment, is one such early decision to consider. Setting limitations on the purchase of the child's wardrobe to a realistic quantity and cost appropriate for the child's age is another of these early investment decisions. To trust a mature guardian as baby-sitter when the infant is still bottle or breast fed so that parents may have some private time together at outside activities is still another. The key point is that the child must be placed in the proper perspective of the family unit, the marriage, and the child's own realistic needs. Priorities must be set and consistently maintained.

2. The parents' wishes, hopes, dreams, and unfulfilled ambitions too often become funneled into the single child. Each parent has goals and ambitions for the child. This milieu creates a background that is dangerous for all concerned. The parents must establish realistic standards and expectations for their child. "Realistic" has a specific and nondiffuse meaning. It requires a careful and honest analysis of the child's capabilities, talents, and interests before establishing goal criteria for the youngster. The only child is not the mirror image of either parent nor is he the amalgamation of all their talents and dreams. He is himself, slowly becoming a totally individualistic and specific person. Parental expectations must be kept at a low-key, rational level during the early years until the child has established the beginnings of his own identity. Premature setting of goals and overly high expectations can only lead to serious frustration for both the parents and the child. Otherwise this will ultimately lead to a sense of continuous failure which may culminate in the child's refusal to attempt the possible, much less accept more difficult challenges. The exhaustion of trying to climb the mountain of unrealistic parental expectations can indeed incapacitate the only child, leaving him at the bottom, gasping in anger, self-pity, and frustration.

As the child grows, he should be included in the process of setting the levels expected of him. His wishes and perceptions of himself and his own potential must be taken into consideration as he matures so that he feels a real sense of participation in his own destiny. It is far easier to accept the standards set by yourself than those imposed by others. The adolescent, during his phase of rebellion, will have less to resist and reject if the expectations and levels of accomplishment result from family discussions at which he is an important contributor.

3. The only child must be allowed to mature at his own pace. Often, the only child will be overexposed to the adult world, its games, conversations, defenses, artifices. These may become behavior models which the only child chooses to emulate. The end result is a premature adult, too wise in his vocabulary, too immature in his understanding, too shaky in his ability to transfer his adult world experiences and language into the quite different world of his own peers. He is playing an adult role for which he is untrained and unsuited. This should be avoided at all costs.

The opposite may also take place. The parents may injure the child by denying him the right to test the limits of his world, to grow within himself and within his peer group. The "babying" of the only child, the overconcern with the development of his independence as possibly threatening, the holding back to prevent the headlong rush into young adulthood, may precipitate the emergence of a youngster who is emotionally crippled by immaturity and fear of the outside world.

Growing up is both an experience and an experiment. The only child must be permitted both. Let him grow up at his own speed, with his own painful, unavoidable experiences, testing his environment with the predictably difficult experiments and trials. Stand by as consultant, advisor, and even guide for the occasionally rough terrain. But do not push, pull, hold back, or impede. Create the proper peer environment, eliminate excessive adult influences but avoid manipulating the child's self-pacing. No two children develop or grow at the same rate.

4. Avoid becoming dependent upon the child for the emotional nourishment and companionship that may otherwise be missing in your own life. Obviously this is an unhealthy situation which can only lead to anxiety over separation, and great parental disappointment as the child attempts to breach the overly tight emotional bonds wound around him.

It is essential that parents establish the clear understanding quite early in their relationship with their child that they have distinctly separate lives from the life of their offspring. Their lives intersect, cross over, and overlap in certain vital areas, but in others are separate, private, individual, and independent. There must be a mutual respect for the differences as well as the similarities. Only through the realization of the independent aspects of his parents' lives will the only child feel comfortable to experiment with the possibilities of developing the private and specific parts of his own. Separation then becomes less of a problem.

The parents must daily strive to create a sense of independence in their child. Not to be needed at some point in the adult life of your child is the unmistakable mark of successful parenting. Not being needed is never to be misinterpreted as not being loved.

5. Parents must encourage and stimulate their youngster to make his own decisions quite early. Should I choose red or yellow for this picture? Should I play with this child or that? Decisions enlarge, grow in complexity, expand in their impact upon the child's final life-style. But only if the ability to make the simplest decisions is developed in the beginning can the child go on to the more intricate personal problem-solving needed in later years. Allowing the child to make his own decisions runs the risk of poor results, failures, the unhappy acceptance of error. But we all live with our own errors, our own failures. We must also learn from them, grow from them, resist committing the same mistake the second time. Only with the ability to decide, to err, to fail, to recover will the only child develop the resiliency necessary to cope with the vagaries of adult life. He cannot be invited to run back to the parents for the constant reassurance of adult opinion, the mature advice, the parental assumption of the decision-making role. As parents, you will not always be around to make those decisions. What will the child do then? To whom could he turn? To husband or wife who will tire of the weakness? To the physician or psychiatrist who will charge for his inability? To a society which will reject the responsibility? The child must make the decisions which will prepare him for the life-long task of solving personal problems. The responsibility to see that this skill and strength is developed in the only child rests upon the shoulders of the parents who must resist the urge to supply the answers.

6. From the time of early childhood, the parents must make available to the only child all forms of peer activity, both group and singular. The only child, because of the lack

of close peer contact within the home, is often by nature or by choice a loner. This must not always be viewed as a handicap; but the child must eventually have the opportunity to choose his peers after a full introduction to all of the forms of peer interactions. Neighborhoods with many other children are preferable for this, of course. However, only children are often urban children because of the nature of their parents' careers, so immediate neighborhood contacts may be limited. Nursery schools and cooperative play groups should then become a part of the only child's early exposure to other peers. It is better if this introduction is not always accompanied by the presence of one or the other parent. The child must learn to adapt to the peer group without the immediate availability of parental support. Give him the chance.

By elementary school age many set patterns of peer expectation and interaction will have developed. Therefore, the parent cannot rely on or wait for elementary school experience to introduce the child to the negotiations and games which he must know if he is to co-exist with peers.

Again, only children will commonly select a single friend, share their emotional lives on an intense basis with this companion, and feel the exquisite pain of loss when the relationship ends. The parent must accept the singleness of these relationships and the possible pain. Interference in these close relationships is an unwarranted parental involvement in a very personal and very private aspect of a child's life. The parent may remain accessible for the counsel and the comfort necessary during such a tight friendship, but advice must be on request only and should not be initiated by the parent. The parents should attempt to disrupt such a friendship only if the friend selected has serious personality problems which the parents honestly assess and feel could be ultimately harmful to their child. Only under these extreme conditions is parental interference in the relationship permissible. Otherwise, no matter how different the existing relationship is from the fantasy friendship models which the parents have for their child, the parents must keep hands off.

7. Parents must be uncompromisingly honest and this honesty must extend to their assessment of their child. No rose-colored glasses are permitted, no illusions allowed. They must consistently view their child, their child's talents and capabilities, their child's activities with the clear vision that permits accurate evaluation. The parents must truthfully and sincerely

acknowledge their only child's faults as well as his virtues, his failures as well as his successes, his weaknesses as well as his talent. Overpraise dilutes the value of the sincere compliment. Insincere assessment weakens the meaning of subsequent critical evaluation. The parent, as critic and counselor, loses credibility when the clarity of vision and honesty of personal reporting and evaluating are lost in the maze of affection and compassion.

To recognize the positive and the negative in the child will enable the parent to assist in the selection of meaningful extra-school activities, as well as future career choices and educational possibilities. Every child should learn the truths about himself gradually in the supportive and comfortable environment of home before facing the unshaded honesty of the outside world. The parents are the only child's sole source of this information. Do not deprive the only child of his slowly dawning self-knowledge within an honest and understanding family unit.

8. The activities of the outside world will not revolve around the only child. Therefore, the activities of the family unit must emulate the outside society and equalize the child-oriented activities with those specifically designed for the two adults in the family unit. The parents must schedule specific events which will exclude the child and be shared by them alone. These may be balanced with the child-centered trips, movies, visits, etc. However, the child must be made fully aware of the fact that his parents have a separate existence, a marriage which demands time and attention, and individual selves that need intermittent private replenishment.

The only child can become a thorn in the side of an otherwise healthy marriage. If all family time is directed toward the centrally focused child, all of the members of the household will suffer as the supporting structure—the marriage—weakens. Further, the adults must remember that very soon the child will have grown and developed a private life from which they at times will be excluded. During these periods (which will increase as the years add up) the couple will have to rely on the strong base for their own relationship or there will be an emptiness, a void in the marriage.

9. Consistent discipline is a necessity in rearing every youngster. It is no less important in the family with one child. However, the very close and delicate relationship in the case of an only child often makes the implementation of consist-

ent discipline extremely difficult for the parents. They may become desperately afraid of overdisciplining. If they have no previous training in child-rearing, the level of appropriate discipline is unknown territory. In addition, they often feel a gnawing fear that if they punish or reprimand their coveted only child, the youngster's love and caring for them will, in some way, be diminished. The thought that they might turn their child against them will often immobilize the parents confronted with the absolute necessity of administering discipline. The result is inconsistent and ineffectual chastening, which only heightens the insecurity of the child who is looking to the parents to set the limits, to point out the danger spots, to draw the lines across which lie social ostracism. Without these guidelines the only child stands alone, facing the world without knowing the rules.

Parents of only children must consider that the parent-child relationship often progresses in sequential fashion. At first the child views the parent with some degree of fear because the parent must assert a definite limit to the life-threatening dangers in early childhood. Without this fear, what keeps the child from running into the street when the mother sharply calls out to halt? This fear is the first guideline which very subtly blends into a feeling of respect for the firmness, the consistency, the good sense of the disciplinary measures of the parent. The love which emanates from this respect is deep and lasting. Thus, the parent who fears the loss of his child's love because of discipline has the truth reversed. The loss will occur as the parent continues to shirk the role of parent which the child demands. Consistent discipline must be present.

10. The single child, when young, is much more susceptible to the magic of fantasy. Times of isolation and loneliness may be filled to the brim by imaginary friends and pets. Anger, fear, or hurt pride can be unleashed without danger of reprisal or harsh judgment from the imaginary friend. Many children will create momentary fantasies to help them through confusing, frightening situations or temporary boredom. But the only child is likely to permit the fantasy world to infiltrate and somewhat influence behavior. The parents have to understand the causes of the fantasy reaction, attempt to subtly correct the excessive periods of isolation and lack of peer contact, and accept the fact of the imaginary as-

pect of the child's world without allowing themselves to become incorporated within it.

The fantasies must be limited. At no time should the parents acknowledge the actuality of the fantasy nor permit its extension into the child's activities outside the home. If the real happenings of life become obsessively replaced by the unreal in the child's daily existence, then the parents must attempt to establish a realistic balance by pointing out to their youngster the need for continuous contact with the actual world. The only child who clings to an imaginary world after the first few years must be viewed less with tolerance and more with concern. By school age the fantasy world should have been passed through or eliminated by interaction with other children in the school environment. If not, then the child should be evaluated very carefully by parent and professional to determine the seriousness of the refusal to give up the imaginary life.

11. Because there is only one child to lavish with attention and elicit responses, the parents may unknowingly find themselves in direct competition with each other for the child's favor and time. This must be avoided at all costs. This puts the child in the unfortunate position of being guilty of denying the other parent. The child will learn manipulative tactics with which to control both adults as a result of the continuous parental vying. No one in the family unit wins in this game.

The parents of the only child must thoughtfully analyze their individual and collective personalities and decide who will do what. There are no firm guidelines as to specific tasks. Many can be jointly shared; others can be changed as the growth of the child suggests that the one parent might better fill the role for the older youth than the parent who had previously accepted the particular assignment. Flexibility must be part of the operational definition of the family unit. One parent has to be willing and capable of stepping in and assuming the tasks of the other. This must not be done on a competitive basis to win the child's approval; it should be a mutually understood and negotiated undertaking by both parents designed to give the youngster a clear understanding of the roles and to discourage manipulations.

12. Every child rebels throughout his growing years. The only child, because of the intensity of focus, may rebel with an extra dash of enthusiasm and vigor. The parent must un-

derstand this need for self-expression and must struggle to maintain and constantly reestablish the standards and regulations bent out of shape experimentally by the child as a means of testing the limits. Understanding the rebellion does not mean accepting the consequences, however. If it appears harmful to the child, another person, or society, then the parent should intervene with a reasonable explanation of the situation. If the rebellion is more internal and forms part of the youngster's development of self, then the parent should allow it to reach the point where the child has experimented, experienced, and learned, but not necessarily done himself any irreparable harm, either emotionally or physically. To quell all rebellions, to refuse to allow the growing child to experiment with breaking a few of life's rules, to obstruct his exploration of views other than those held by the parents—to be so rigid—is to restrict the emotional and social growth of the child.

13. Parents must be very careful not to overkill the emphasis on creativity within their child. Saturation blurs the vision and dulls the appetite. It becomes important for the parent to assess what the child enjoys doing, where his talents appear to lie, and what the child's physical skills realistically permit. The decision as to which activity will be tried, and when, should be a joint one. The parents must remember that their child is a different and quite specific individual whose interests may not gravitate toward theirs.

The choice often made by the child is with the inherent knowledge of his own capabilities. Again here the parent should act as stimulus, catalyst, advisor, and counselor. When it becomes apparent that the child has lost interest in the specific activity or has determined himself to be less than talented in the particular area, the parent should not press for the child to persevere. The final wisdom may very well rest within the decision of the child. He knows himself, better than anyone else, his capabilities and limitations.

14. The external, superficial rewards of winning often attract the only child who has an accentuated need for approval. The desires to be best, the brightest, the most beautiful become goals that the only child sets for himself without the realization that the most important rewards are internal. As the child grows, the stress on external accolades should be minimized, and the emphasis placed upon the self-satisfaction and gratification that one receives from knowing that a job

has been undertaken, completed, and accomplished to the best of one's ability. If the parent can impart this to the child, then the years of frustration, of constantly seeking the evanescent approval of the crowd, will be avoided.

15. The health and body image of the only child must not be given unnatural stress and emphasis. The parents' unconscious transmission of the sense of impending loss and fear with each minor childhood illness creates an exaggerated awareness of the body and its vulnerability, leading to hypochondriacal symptoms and occasionally malingering or the use of illness as a manipulative device within the family unit and, eventually, the outer social world. Whether it be injury or illness the parents must train themselves to treat any deviations from normal within the child's body as a normal biologic phenomenon rather than an impending threat to the family foundation. A rational approach to health and body are essential if the child is to grow into a well-adjusted adult who can communicate realistically and appropriately with medical professionals. Overconcern regarding illness and overemphasis on matters of body integrity will result in the emergence of a neurotic adult who lives with constant anxiety about his body and health. Medical people can help the parent in this regard by their calm and thoughtful discussions with the child during the time of illness or injury or surgery. The parents must reinforce this calm by bringing an assured attitude and manner to the child's bedside.

16. One of the most important tasks of the parent is that of sex educator. The more the adult knows and understands, the more comfortable will be the subject when raised by the child. No matter how close the parent-child relationship, no parent has the prerogative of abrogating his or her responsibility as education consultant to his or her child in the area of sexual information.

The child should be permitted first to explore and know his own body, having all of his early questions sensibly and realistically answered on a level which he can understand. With normal curiosity, the child will usually then explore the aspects of his parents' bodies by being around when the parents undress or bathe. Again, an unashamed approach and acceptance of the child's curiosity with the proper responses to the multiple questions will move the child toward a natural and full understanding of the normal variations in human sexuality and intimate behavior. Ultimately, with the aid of books, pictures, and other media, and using a comfortable approach, the parents will be responsible for the progressive and total education of their child in the subject of sexual behavior. The teacher, the priest or rabbi, the physician, and others may lend assistance, but the ultimate responsibility lies with the parents.

17. Because of the focus upon the single child within the family and the subsequent tendency to permit the only child to cast a major vote in family decisions and policy, the child learns the quality of dominance quite early in his life. The parent of the only child must be extremely careful that this sense, this feeling of control, is properly integrated into the communal family situation and not allowed to grow out of proportion. Otherwise the child will likely carry this sense of overt control into peer and other adult relationships only to find rejection and dismissal. At no time can the roles be reversed. Never should the youngster's control create a situation whereby the child rules as if he were the parent. It is a subtle and gradual take-over by the only child, responding to what he perceives is the unspoken family plan. This must be prevented, and, if unwittingly developing, nipped in the bud as quickly as possible.

18. The parents of the only child cannot force feed what is best for the child. The child must select what he finds acceptable and attractive from all of the concepts, philosophies, and plans. He may move away from the total family structure and training for a period of time in order to gain a more objective perspective. This critical period of analysis and controlled experimentation should be permitted by the parents. Obviously, no child should be compelled to be what the parents have programmed him to be. The only child runs the highest risk of such programming; therefore, parents must concentrate not on what the only child will make of himself as far as career or future is concerned, but should direct their energies into the consummate human being their only child will become. Their focus should be on his caring for the other person, his ability to communicate, his adjustment to life and its daily crises, his contentment with himself, and his fulfillment as a productive human being. Those characteristics are essentially what is truly "best" for him.

19. Very simply stated, the only child must not become involved in any marital conflicts on a daily or long-term basis. The child must never be used as a pawn in the parents' dis-

agreements. The foundation of the family unit must be firm for the child, no matter how shaky the marriage. Even to the point of parental separation or divorce, the only child must have the inherent sense that these two people have separated from each other but not from him. The role of father and mother must continue to be played no matter at which diverse locations or whether performed in unison or as separate forces. The introduction of new characters into the family drama as stepparents does not eliminate the necessity for both natural parents to maintain their responsibilities as such.

20. As the only child is very clearly the center of attention within the family, this must be controlled so as not to have the star quality get out of hand. If one adds the situation of adoption or a handicapping condition to the only child, the risk of undiluted, pressurized, overemphatic parental focusing on the child increases by multiples. If the only child has been adopted, the preceding nineteen points stand firmly as a foundation for the new relationship. If the only child has a handicap, there are no leniency factors permitting the parents to abandon these same tenets. Permissiveness and refusal to recognize the need for controls will often only cripple the child more than the handicap ever could. Neither an adoption nor a handicapping condition should add the burden of being special to the rearing of the only child. In both situations, minimize the uniqueness of the child and concentrate on the aspects of child-rearing which relate to the development of the total human being, and not merely one single aspect.

PRESCRIPTIONS FOR GRANDPARENTS

This book would not be complete without a few prescriptions for grandparents, as they often play a significant role in the lives of their only grandchildren. This role may be a positive one filled with the beauty and love of a healthy grandparent-grandchild relationship. On the other hand, the grandparent may create havoc within the home of the only child by interference, innuendo, and refusal to play the grandparent role.

1. Relax and enjoy it. Being a grandparent is one of the most satisfying conditions known to man if the grandparent can only accept the role. The disciplining is no longer the responsibility of the older person. The illnesses will be taken

care of by the parents. The bills, the fights, the problems are not the grandparents' primary concern. They may be called in as elder statespersons for opinions and advice, but the immediate solutions and decisions are not essentially theirs. What they possess is the opportunity to enjoy their grandchildren, to love them, play with them—to give and receive without the total responsibility of parenthood. When things get rough, most grandparents have the capability of handing the screaming baby, the misbehaving two-year-old, or the disrespectful five-year-old back into the arms of the parents, smile resignedly and silently leave, making plans to return another day when child behavior is more tolerable. If they have given their own children the proper models of parenting, then the problems should be solved during the period of their absence.

2. Grandparents are greater spoilers than parents. The grandparents of the only child must be very careful not to innundate the child with gifts or affection or trips. Controls on the grandparents' enthusiasm must be maintained or the most assiduous attempts to rear a well-adjusted, well-disciplined only child will be undermined and possibly even destroyed. The best advice for the grandparent of the only child is, do not do and do not buy without first checking with the child's parents. This is essential to the maintenance of a warm relationship between grandparent and parent and the avoidance of the emergence of competitive interaction between the two generations for the attention and obedience and affection of the only child.

3. The only child already has two parents. He doesn't need two more. What he really would like is two grandparents. Grandparents must always bear in mind who are the parents and the authority figures. He cannot have two sets of parents, two sets of role models. The grandparents who attempt to take over the rearing create an internally confusing and frightening dilemma within the child. Namely, he begins to question the competence of his own mother and father. He wonders and then agonizes. He ricochets off the bickering influences of grandparent vs. parent, trying not to take sides or mediate the arguments. In this game for assumption of control the loser will be the only child. The grandparents have had their turn at parenting; they must constantly keep in perspective who the disciplinarians and decision-makers are. And they are relinquishing a wonderful experience if

they refuse to accept the limitations but also the opportunities of the grandparent role.

There are no perfect parents, no more than there are perfect children. We are all fallible. We all make mistakes. Occasional mistakes in parenting will not result in a seriously damaged child. It is only the continuous and consistent errors that leave their permanent imprint. Many of these are, in reality, scars which only psychiatry or counseling over a long period can hope to erase. The way to avoid this is to practice preventive parenting, to be aware of the danger signals, the warning signs, the treacherous age periods and events, the possible alternative solutions, and finally and most importantly, the appropriate methods of child-rearing. These should be assimilated and discussed in advance so that every effort can be made to create the most emotionally and physically healthful environment in which the child can grow. This is the essence of preventive parenting.

The only child presents a challenge. For years, the thought of an only-child family immediately brought to mind the picture of a disturbed and unhappy parent-child relationship and the emergence of a malcontented, maladapted only-child adult. There is no rationale or need for this to be the case. Rearing the only child can be an exciting and fulfilling experience for both parents. The only child can grow, thrive, flourish and enter adulthood adjusted, contented and capable of maintaining a life full of satisfaction and productivity. The ingredients are within the family unit.

Read the foregoing prescriptions slowly and carefully. Select those which fit and apply them to the parent-child relationship. This may prevent injury. Or, if the injury has already occurred, use the appropriate prescription and watch for healing. Gradually, the prescriptions will become an integral part of the parents' solutions, a personal pharmacy of answers which have proven helpful and workable therapies in the past. At that point, a professional parent has developed. But most of all, the parent of the only child has realized that raising the only child requires a combination of good sense, information, comfort, joy, love, and the knowledge that, with the correct parenting approach, the only child can become a happy, fully adjusted member of society, totally indistinguishable from his peers and far removed from the old, negative stereotype.

About the Author

Dr. Murray Kappelman graduated summa cum laude from the University of Maryland Medical School. After two years of service in the U. S. Army Medical Corps, he became chief resident in pediatrics at University Hospital in Baltimore. He was in private practice from 1960 through 1967 and is presently professor of pediatrics at the University of Maryland Medical School and assistant professor of pediatrics at Johns Hopkins Medical School.

Author of *What Your Child Is All About,* Dr. Kappelman has also contributed articles to such nationally known magazines as *Family Health* and *Glamour,* as well as numerous medical journals.

More SIGNET Books of Special Interest

☐ **YOU AND YOUR BABY: A Guide to Pregnancy, Birth and the First Year by Dr. Frederick W. Rutherford.** A practical handbook for new parents that tells them everything they need to know about pregnancy, preparation for the baby as well as the emotional and physical development of the average infant in his first year.
(#E8417—$2.95)

☐ **LIFE BEFORE BIRTH by Ashley Montagu. Revised edition.** Vital information for the mother-to-be to increase her chances of bearing a normal, healthy baby. Introduction by Dr. Alan F. Guttmacher. (#J8239—$1.95)

☐ **PREPARATION FOR CHILDBIRTH: A Lamaze Guide by Donna and Rodger Ewy.** Here is the book to instruct prospective parents in the Lamaze techniques for easier childbirth, complete with diagrams and photographs outlining each sequence from labor through delivery. "Excellent . . . provides the necessary tools for a self-controlled, shared childbirth experience."—The Bookmark (#J7476—$1.95)

☐ **PLEASE BREAST FEED YOUR BABY by Alice Gerard.** A fascinating look at the latest scientific findings on the benefits of breast-feeding for both mother and child and a simple, helpful guide to make nursing easy and successful. (#W7868—$1.50)

☐ **NATURAL PARENTHOOD: Raising Your Child Without a Script by Eda J. LeShan.** Here is a positive approach to the pain and the pleasure of being a parent and the right to raise your child as you see fit.
(#Y7762—$1.25)

☐ **PREGNANCY, BIRTH AND FAMILY PLANNING by Dr. Alan F. Guttmacher.** Written especially for today's expectant and potential parents—the most comprehensive, comforting, and fact-filled guide ever published. The one necessary total guide for expectant parents in the 1970's. (#E8316—$2.25)

SIGNET Books for Your Reference Shelf

Other SIGNET Books of Interest